DIFFERENTIATION MADE SIMPLE
TIMESAVING TOOLS FOR TEACHERS

MARY ANN CARR

PRUFROCK PRESS INC.
WACO, TEXAS

Prufrock Press Inc.
P.O. Box 8813
Waco, TX 76714-8813
Phone: (800) 998-2208
Fax: (800) 240-0333
http://www.prufrock.com

To my loving husband and partner, David

CONTENTS

INTRODUCTION

THINK of this book as a toolkit filled with practical tools you can use every day to differentiate in language arts, social studies, and science in grades 4–8. Differentiation is a practice that is beneficial to every student. Rather than focus on leaving no child behind, differentiation aims to move every child ahead. All students—struggling learners, gifted, and those on grade level—soar when challenged by work appropriate for their abilities, interests, and learning styles.

As a gifted and talented resource teacher and consultant in various school systems, I sought to help classroom teachers overcome obstacles to differentiation. Some found the task overwhelming and became frustrated; a few gave up. No wonder. Designing differentiated lessons, activities, learning centers, and units is a time-consuming effort—and time is a precious commodity, especially to a teacher.

Taking time pressures into account as well as other key questions and concerns that teachers voiced, I began to develop materials to help make their task easier. This toolkit is a compilation of these materials. In order to be included in the kit, a tool had to meet the following criteria:

- the tool had to save teachers time;
- it had to address teachers' key questions and concerns regarding differentiation (see Table 1); and
- the tools that utilize questions, activities, or task cards had to be generic so they could be used in a variety of ways.

This toolkit is for the practitioner, not the academician. Therefore, it does not include a discussion of theory. It does not attempt to define, describe, or

Table I
Teacher Questions and Tools That Address Them

Teacher Questions	Tools That Address Them	Chapter
• If I want to differentiate, how do I get started?	• Strategies to Prepare Students for Differentiation	I
• How do I get students to understand why some of them might be doing activities that are different from the rest of the class?	• This is Me Graph	I
• What if one group of students wants to do what another group is doing but they aren't capable of doing it?	• Strategies to Prepare Students for Differentiation	I
• How do students accept the fact that they all have different skills and abilities without feeling either superior or inferior to others?	• Strategies to Prepare Students for Differentiation • This is Me Graph	I
• How can I have different students working on different topics at the same time when there is only one of me in the class?	• Guidelines for Successful Groups • Generic Anchor Activities	2
• What if students are unable to work in groups or independently?	• Guidelines for Successful Groups • Generic Anchor Activities	2
• What if students misbehave while working in groups or alone?	• Guidelines for Successful Groups	2
• How can I vary questions in order to challenge my gifted and bright students and yet ask questions that my struggling learners can answer without getting frustrated?	• Tiered Questions • Tic-Tac-Toe Menus	3
• How can I create tiered lessons when I have limited planning time?	• Tiered Questions • Tic-Tac-Toe Menus	3
• What can I use instead of workbooks and worksheets to accompany my units?	• Literature Graphic Organizers • Digging Deeper With Bloom	3
• How can I create differentiated lessons and activities to accompany the trade books and stories my students are reading in language arts?	• A Guide to Developing Differentiated Units for Trade Books and Short Stories • A Grand Conversation • Book Projects	3
• How can I differentiate vocabulary study in my classroom?	• Tiered Activities for Vocabulary Study • Vocabulary Graphic Organizers	3
• How can I create learning centers on a variety of topics when I have so little time?	• Generic Task Cards for Differentiated Learning Center	4
• How can I develop learning center activities that reflect different skill levels?	• Generic Task Cards for Differentiated Learning Center	4
• How can I develop a writing center that will be motivating to my students?	• Creative Writing Learning Center Guide	4
• How can I develop task cards for a creative writing center that I can use throughout the year?	• Creative Writing Task Cards	4
• How can I encourage students to edit the stories they write?	• Student Editing Guide	4
• How can I get my bright students involved and excited about an independent research project when I have to spend so much of my time working with my struggling learners?	• The Research Folder Strategy: Ten Steps to Independent Research	5

Teacher Questions	Tools That Address Them	Chapter
• How can I assign independent research projects when my students don't know how to organize such a project?	• The Research Folder Strategy: Ten Steps to Independent Research • Task Cards for Independent Research	5
• How can I keep students from copying information from Web sites and other sources when they're working on a report?	• The Research Folder Strategy: Ten Steps to Independent Research	5
• How can I differentiate products when I have little time to plan?	• Product List	6
• How do I assess student products that are open-ended and subjective?	• Four Generic Rubrics	6
• I want to use rubrics but when can I find the time to develop them?	• Four Generic Rubrics • Conversion Tables	6

establish a rationale for differentiation. These items are addressed in many other resources, and I have listed my favorite ones in the back of this book (see pp. 135–136).

This toolkit was designed especially for the teacher in the trenches, challenged daily to meet the diverse needs of all students in the classroom. Glance at Table 1 for questions you might have and then browse through the book and select all of the tools that you can start using today.

Use this book if you:

■ are interested in differentiating your instruction but have not yet tried it. "The Tools to Get Started" in the first chapter and the "Classroom Management Tools" in the second chapter will guide you and encourage you to take that first step;

■ are a pro at differentiation but find that shortage of time is a deterrent;

■ are creative and want to develop original units with differentiated questions and activities;

■ want to develop differentiated activities to accompany chapters in the students' textbook;

■ want to develop supplemental activities for your gifted students who complete assignments ahead of the class;

■ want to develop learning centers featuring topics you are studying or topics of student interest;

■ want your students to develop research skills for independent projects; or

■ want to differentiate products and assess each one using rubrics.

I once asked a group of students what the world would be like if we were all the same. One boy commented dryly, "Aren't we? At school, anyway."

The student's response jarred me. Then I remembered my first image of a classroom, one that had encouraged me to begin teacher training. It was a classroom filled with children with 10-year-old minds, 10-year-old abilities, 10-year-old behaviors, and 10-year-old ideas—a collective blur of bodies as eager to learn, as I was to teach them.

It never occurred to me the real classroom I would find. The students, all 10 years old perhaps, but all of them unique in every other respect: their abilities, knowledge, interests, motivation, ideas, thoughts, and dreams. It didn't take me long to realize a classroom is as diverse as the world in which we live.

It is this diversity that drives differentiation. I encourage you to use the tools in this book to help you address these differences, enabling all of your students to reach their potential.

CHAPTER I

TOOLS TO GET STARTED

PRIOR to taking the first step to differentiate in your classroom, it is important to prepare your students for differentiation. It is essential that your students understand that not everyone will always be doing the same thing at the same time. It is equally important for them to understand why. Guide them to recognize and appreciate the differences within the classroom. Explain that everyone has different abilities, interests, and learning styles. Point out that it is fortunate everyone is different and brings different gifts to the table.

Use the strategies included here early in the school year. These strategies will help establish a classroom environment supportive of differentiation by promoting positive attitudes about student differences.

STRATEGIES TO PREPARE
STUDENTS FOR DIFFERENTIATION

Play Four Corners

This game will make it visibly clear that not everyone in the classroom is alike. To play, ask a multiple-choice question with four possible answers. Designate four corners of the room and tell students to indicate their answer by standing in one of these corners. For example, you might ask, "What is your favorite subject in school? If it is reading, stand in this corner. If it is math, stand in that corner; if it is social studies, that one; and if it is science, stand in the fourth corner."

After asking the question, direct students to walk quietly to the corner of their choice. Make it clear that students are not to run or talk to one another during this activity, but carefully observe what choices their classmates make. You will want to ask the students several questions, repeating the above process, before sending students back to their seats and discussing what they've observed in the activity.

Possible questions for this game that would reveal information about students include:

- Would you rather draw, read, write, or build something?
- What noun best describes you: historian, mathematician, scientist, or writer?
- Would you rather work alone? With a partner? A small group? The whole class?
- Before you write a story or report, do you prefer to use a web or other graphic organizer to brainstorm ideas? An outline? A sketch? Or, do you just like to start writing without a plan?
- Are you at your best mentally in the early morning, early afternoon, late afternoon, or evening?

After each question, ask students to look around and see who is standing in each corner. After the game, discuss their observations about the differences within the classroom. Ask if the people standing in certain corners surprised anyone.

If one or two students stand alone in a corner, take the opportunity to praise them for being individuals and not feeling the need to follow the crowd. Model your respect for students who have the strength to stand up for who they are even when it means they stand alone.

This Is Me Graph

On the board, list eight abilities related to school, such as reading, spelling, writing stories, solving word problems, and conducting science experiments or research. Hand out the This Is Me graph (see p. 4). Instruct students to copy the list of abilities onto the bottom row of the graph. Ask them to indicate on the graph how competent they are in each area, using a scale of 1 to 10. After students have completed their graphs, display them. Discuss patterns they see in the graphs, and list these on the board. Lead students to discover that everyone has different strengths and weaknesses.

Fairness Slogans

Teach the slogan, "Fair doesn't mean doing the same thing." Write a difficult word to spell on the board, and ask students if it would be fair to make students learn that word and others like it if they were weak in spelling. Lead the students in a class discussion.

Then, write a super easy word on the board and ask if it would be just as unfair to ask a super speller to learn to spell this word. Discuss how this would be a waste of the student's time. You might do the same with math problems or a reading passage. Teach this slogan: "Fair is learning something new every day."

Explain that because everyone has different strengths and weaknesses, they should not all be expected to do the same thing in school all of the time. Explain that sometimes during the day, students might be working on different activities or have different assignments that are appropriate for their ability. If students complain that someone is doing something that looks too easy, say, "Remember our slogan, 'Fair doesn't mean doing the same thing.'" Or, if students see a bright child working on an independent study and beg to do the same thing, again refer to the slogan.

If students want to try an assignment that they see others doing, and you think they might be successful, let them do it. If you know the assignment would be too difficult, however, lead them to another activity that would be more appropriate for their ability. Explain that this work is just as important as the assignments other students are doing.

This Is Me Graph

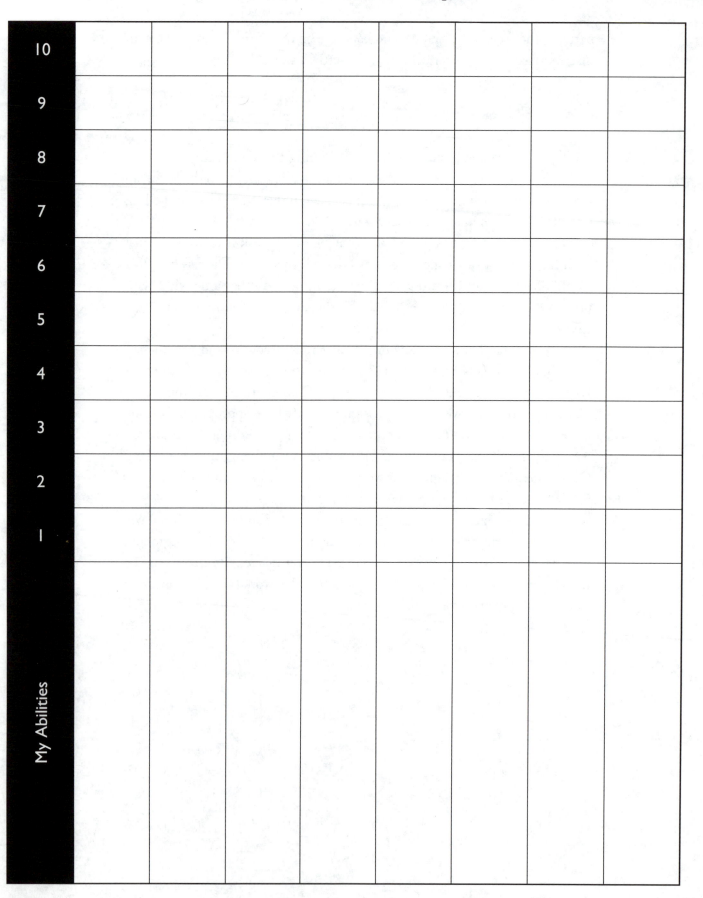

10							
9							
8							
7							
6							
5							
4							
3							
2							
1							
My Abilities							

CHAPTER 2

CLASSROOM MANAGEMENT TOOLS

THE first step in managing a differentiated classroom is to train students to work independently and in groups. They must be reminded to stay on task, keep their voices down, and not distract their neighbors. This training takes patience. Yet, it pays off and will eventually enable you to manage your class with ease. The Guidelines for Successful Groups (see p. 6) provide ideas for establishing a classroom environment conducive to students working in small groups.

Anchors are useful management tools. They are activities given to the whole class or a small group, usually at the beginning of a class period. While one group of students is working on an anchor, you are free to meet with another group for instruction, assessment, or to give directions for another type of activity you have assigned.

Reading, journal writing, creative writing, practicing skills (e.g., spelling, alphabetizing, punctuation), or a "problem of the day" are examples of anchor activities. All students may complete the same activity or there may be two or three, focusing on different levels of readiness.

If the activities are open-ended, there is less need to differentiate the task because students can complete the task according to their ability. The following are examples of open-ended activities:

- How many words can you make using these letters?
- Use vocabulary words to write a short story.
- Make a list of all the words you could use instead of "said".

Use the list of Generic Anchor Activities (see p. 8) when you need an anchor and have little time to plan one. Choose an anchor and think how you might fill in the blank with words related to a topic you're studying. Write the anchor on the board or a poster and ask students to come up with as many answers as they can.

GUIDELINES FOR SUCCESSFUL GROUPS

1. Give yourself time before you begin using groups. Never use groups until you have all other areas of classroom management in place, such as talking one at a time, listening, following directions, and the like. After your students learn what is expected of them in whole-class instruction, they are ready to begin training to work in groups.

2. To train students, set high standards for groups. For group success, students should focus on:
   - getting materials and putting them away,
   - finding places for completed work,
   - using behaviors appropriate for group work, and
   - using "secret" voices (the volume you would use when telling a friend a secret).

3. Establish rules for working with partners, in groups, and at centers. Be consistent in enforcing consequences when rules are broken. Rules for groups might include the following:
   - When working in a group or with a partner, use "secret" voices.
   - Work quietly so you will not bother those working around you.
   - Whether you are working alone or in a group, remember—*you* are responsible for staying on task and for getting the job done.
   - If you have a question, try to figure it out on your own. Use what you already know to help you. You also may use any resources you may have (including class notes, textbooks, and posters in the classroom).
   - "Ask *three* before you ask me." If you cannot answer a question on your own, you should always ask three fellow students before asking the teacher. (One student can be designated a "daily expert" to help field student questions about the assignment.)

- If you complete the activity, check it carefully and make changes if necessary. Then, find something constructive to do. (Teachers would be wise to have supplementary materials on hand for students who finish early.)

4. If groups get too loud, say, "Lights out!" or "Freeze!" Then, give students one minute to calm down, reflect, and change their behavior. When they get it together, allow them to start working again.

5. If one or more groups are disruptive, identify another group that is working successfully. Praise that group: "I like the way this group is working quietly and on task." Positive reinforcement of the successful group usually influences the others to get under control.

6. Prior to sitting down with a small group, always remind the other students they are not to ask you questions. You may use hats, signs, or hand signals as cues for students not to interrupt: "When I'm wearing this hat, do not approach me." Despite your efforts to prevent it, if students do interrupt, hold up your hand and say, "Are you hurt? Sick? Is anyone bleeding? If not, please sit down and I'll be with you when I'm finished."

7. Train students what to do when they are unsure about how to complete a task, rather than interrupting you. Make a poster that reads:

Things You Can Do Instead of Asking Me:
- Use your resources.
- Ask three before you ask me: ask a friend, a partner in your group, or the daily expert.
- Skip it until you can get help and go on to another problem or task.

8. If students are disruptive while working in a group, remove them from the group and have them complete the assignment alone.

9. If a student working alone on a differentiated assignment is disruptive, have him return to the whole group if you are teaching the class. If you are working with a small group, have the disruptive student go to "time out" or move him to another area of the room.

10. If a student working alone on a differentiated assignment does not stay on task, have her return to the task the other students in the class are doing.

Generic Anchor Activities

- How many words can you make using the letters in this word: _____.

- How many words can you make using these letters: _____?

- How many ways can you say _____?

- How many ways can you group these words: _____?

- Make a list of words that relate to _____.

- The answer is _____. What is the question?

- Make a list of things that belong in this category: _____.

- What _____ best describes _____ (color, animal, location, food, etc.)? Why is this a good description?

- What if you combined these two things: _____ + _____? What would you have? Name it. Describe its attributes.

- How would you design a new _____?

- What might _____ think about _____? Explain your answer.

- What might _____ say to _____? Write a conversation the two might have, or draw a cartoon using speech balloons.

- What solutions would you suggest for _____?

- List the criteria you would use to judge _____.

- How would you rank order these: _____(five vocabulary or spelling words, five elements of a topic you're studying, five events in your life)?

- What is the best thing about _____? The worst?

- List problems we might have if _____ didn't exist in the world.

- Brainstorm a list of how things might be if we didn't know about _____.

CHAPTER 3
GENERIC QUESTIONS AND ACTIVITIES

VARYING questions and activities is an important strategy in differentiation. Questions that are open-ended and reflect complexity of thought are gems to challenge bright students. Struggling learners, on the other hand, might find these high-level questions frustrating and become discouraged. Questions that focus on the basics are more appropriate for these students. In other words, one question or one series of questions don't always work for the whole class.

As a teacher, you rarely have enough time to do all of the things you need to do. How can you come up with a variety of questions to use in your lessons when you have many different lessons to plan for each day? The tools in this chapter provide lists of questions and activities you can use when designing your lessons, activities, and units. The questions are generic and can be used with a variety of topics in language arts, social studies, and science.

Tiered questions (see p. 10) are helpful tools to use when differentiating a unit or chapter in a textbook. The tiers can accommodate a variety of ability levels in a heterogeneous classroom.

Tic-Tac-Toe (see p. 11) is a tool that allows for student choice and accommodates different ability levels and interests. Students are given a menu of activities. Using the menu, they "win" when they complete three activities in a row, column, or diagonal, as in a game of Tic-Tac-Toe.

A Guide to Developing Differentiated Units for Trade Books and Short Stories (see p. 18) is a tool that can save you time by helping you develop a literature unit based on a trade book or short story. It provides lists of questions, activities, and projects appropriate for a variety of readiness levels and interests. As a result, you can differentiate the activities in the unit even if your students are all reading the same book or story.

This chapter also includes a comprehensive list of book projects you can assign after students complete a book or story, various graphic organizers students can use to organize their thinking about what they have read, and lists of questions you might use in a "grand conversation" (see p. 29). Digging Deeper With Bloom (see p. 31) contains a list of questions pertaining to literature based on Bloom's Revised taxonomy. You can use these to create worksheets to accompany a book chapter or story.

Tiered Activities for Vocabulary Study (see p. 41) is an essential tool if you want to differentiate your vocabulary study. The activities were designed to help you assign differentiated activities to your students even if all of them have the same vocabulary list. This section includes graphic organizers.

TIERED QUESTIONS

Designed in tiers, this tool (see Table 2) provides activities and questions geared for specific groups of students. One tier challenges advanced learners, requiring high-level thinking in order to deal with complexities and make abstractions relating to the topic. The second tier is more appropriate for students working on grade level. The third tier provides still another alternative to approaching the content for struggling learners.

The tiered questions are arranged in sets. Each set focuses on a specific skill required for answering the question, and each one contains three questions of varying difficulty. The continuum of difficulty ranges from "A," the least complex, least abstract, and more structured questions, to "C," the most complex, abstract, and open-ended questions. When planning a tiered activity, choose one to five sets that are appropriate for the topic you're studying. Write the "A" questions from the five sets on one sheet of paper, and copy the page and hand it out to your "A" group. Do the same with the "B" and "C" groups.

The questions in each set contain a blank. The blanks can be filled in with any noun pertaining to the topic you're studying. Consider the following examples.

A. Complete a web about *butterflies*.

B. List the facts you know about *butterflies*. How would you group the facts on your list?

C. Outline what you know about *butterflies*.

A. How is the *Nile River* like the *Amazon*? How are they different?

B. What is most like the *Nile River*? How are they similar? How are they different?

C. How is the *Nile River* like a *major highway*? How are they similar? How are they different?

A. Make a timeline to illustrate major events in the *First Battle of Bull Run*.

B. Compare the sequence of major events in the *First Battle of Bull Run* with the sequence of events in *Battle of Gettysburg*.

C. List three major events in the *First Battle of Bull Run*. If you eliminated one of these events, how might it change the timeline? Make up the new timeline.

TIC-TAC-TOE

This Tic-Tac-Toe tool provides three tiered menus (see pp. 15–17). They range from the least complex, least abstract, and most straightforward questions on Menu 1, to the most complex, abstract, and open-ended questions on Menu 3.

You can use the Tic-Tac-Toe menus in a variety of ways:

■ as a tiered activity in lieu of worksheets to reinforce the main concepts and key ideas of a unit or chapter,

■ as an alternative to unit or chapter questions for students who have already mastered the content,

■ as an alternate activity for students who have compacted out of a chapter, or

■ as a tool of exploration for students who want to explore a topic of their own choosing.

You can make copies of each menu and put them in a sheet protector. This allows you to use the menus over again and again.

Table 2
Tiered Questions

Set	Skill Required to Answer Question	Continuum of Difficulty
1	Collects Data	A. Define _____. B. Describe _____. C. List the characteristics of _____.
2	Collects Data	A. List at least five facts about _____. B. Make a K-W-L chart about _____. C. List at least five questions you have about _____. Then, find the answers to your questions.
3	Organizes Data	A. Make a web about _____. B. List the facts you know about _____. How might you group these facts? C. Outline what you know about _____.
4	Classifies Data	A. Put _____ into a group. List other things that belong in this group. Name the group. B. Think of three groups in which _____ would fit. Name these groups. C. Make a web with _____ as one of the subtopics.
5	Compares/ Contrasts Data	A. How is _____ like _____? How are they different? Show your answer in a Venn diagram. B. Who or what is _____ most like? What makes them so similar? In what ways are they different? C. How is _____ like _____ (a noun from a different topic or discipline)? How are the two different?
6	Illustrates Data	A. Draw a picture of _____. B. Draw _____ in an appropriate setting. Put details in your drawing. C. Draw _____. Include in your drawing at least five props or accessories that are relevant to _____.
7	Looks at Data From Different Perspectives	A. Draw a picture of _____, looking at it from the back. Draw a side view. Draw a picture of how it might look to an eagle flying above it. B. Draw a picture of how _____ might look if you took it apart. Draw each part and label it. C. Picture _____ in your mind's eye. Zoom in on one small part of it. Draw that part. What might that part think about _____? Write the thought balloon in your drawing.
8	Sequences Events	A. Make a timeline to illustrate major events in _____'s existence. B. Compare the sequence of major events in _____'s existence with the sequence of events in _____'s life. Show your answers in a compare/contrast chart. C. List three major events in _____'s existence. If you eliminated one of these events, how might it change the timeline? Develop the new timeline.

Set	Skill Required to Answer Question	Continuum of Difficulty
9	Creates Symbols	A. Draw a symbol to illustrate _____. Explain why this is a good symbol. B. Design a book jacket that could be used for a book about _____. Include at least one symbol in the design. C. Draw an insignia for a Coat of Arms for _____. Include three symbols in the insignia that illustrate characteristics of _____.
10	Imagines Other Uses for an Object	A. Describe how _____ is used. How else might it be used? List as many other uses as you can. B. What might have been used in the past to accomplish the same task as _____? Describe how it was used then. How else might it have been used? List as many other uses as you can. C. What might replace _____ in the future? Describe it. Explain how it might work and how it will accomplish the same task that _____ now accomplishes. Give evidence to support an argument that this is a logical replacement.
11	Makes Predictions	A. Predict what might happen if _____. Give reasons why you think this might happen. B. Predict what might happen if _____. What action might alter the outcome? How might this action be prevented? C. Predict what might happen if _____. What is a similar situation, event, or experiment where this same prediction might be true? Explain.
12	Analyzes	A. What if you took _____ apart? List the main parts and label them. B. What if you took _____ apart? List the main parts. Choose two of these parts, and tell how each one is used (its function). Compare/contrast the functions of these two parts in a Venn diagram. C. What if you took _____ apart? List the main parts. Think about how each part is used. Choose two of these parts, and describe how each one could be used as a part of something else.
13	Analyzes	A. What if you took _____ apart? Select one of its parts. How might _____ be changed if this part were omitted from it? Draw _____ without this part. B. What if you took _____ apart? Select one of its parts. How might _____ be changed if this part was enlarged? Draw _____ with this part enlarged. C. What if you turned _____ inside out? Draw a picture. Explain how _____ would be affected.
14	Personifies Object	A. Draw a scene in which _____ would feel at home. Put many details in your drawing that tell about the scene. B. Draw a scene in which _____ would be most entertained. Explain why it would enjoy this setting. C. Draw an obstacle course through which _____ would have difficulty passing. (However, it could overcome the obstacles and successfully reach the end.) Explain why the obstacles would be difficult for _____.

Set	Skill Required to Answer Question	Continuum of Difficulty
15	Personifies Object	A. What might _____ say to _____? Write a conversation they might have. B. What might _____ feel strongly about? Explain the feeling and why _____ might have it. C. If _____ could talk, what might it say about its environment? Why would it say that?
16	Infers Points of View	A. If _____ could talk, what might it tell you about itself? What frightens it? What makes it angry? Explain your answers. B. What might _____ feel strongly about? Explain why. C. What might others think about _____? Explain your ideas.
17	Infers Points of View	A. What might _____ think about _____? Explain. B. Who might not like _____? Explain why. C. What might people in a different time period think about _____? Why might they think this?
18	Evaluates Object	A. What is _____'s most important feature? Why is it so important? B. What are the three best things about _____? What are three things that are not so great? C. What criteria would you use to judge _____?
19	Evaluates Object	A. What do you like about _____? What do you not like? Why? B. What are the most important contributions _____ has made to the world or to the story? Explain. C. What if _____ had never existed? How would things be different? Explain.
20	Creates New Data	A. What if you combined _____ with _____? Draw a diagram of how the combined objects might look. Tell how this new object might be used. B. How might you change something about _____ to make it better than what it was designed to do or be? Draw a diagram of _____ after the change. Describe the improvement. C. Substitute something for one or more parts of _____ that would change how it might be used. Draw a diagram of the new object and explain its new function (use).

Note. The "A" activities are the least complex, least abstract, and most structured set. The "B" set includes activities of medium complexity, abstractness, and structure. The "C" set include the activities that are most complex, abstract, and open-ended.

Tic-Tac-Toe Menu I

Describe Use as many of your senses as you can to describe your topic.	**Justify** List at least five reasons why you should learn about your topic.	**Categorize** Put your topic in a group and name the group. List the other members of the group.
Divide Tell how you might divide your topic into parts.	**Define** Explain what your topic is.	**Praise** Tell what is good about your topic.
Remember Make a list of at least 10 things that you remember about your topic.	**Associate** What things come to your mind when you think about your topic?	**Web** Make a web with your topic in the center.

Directions: Choose three activities in a row, column, or diagonal about your topic. The topic may be one your teacher selected, or one you may be asked to choose. It might be an event, an animal, a person, a place, an object, an invention, a story plot, or a concept (such as freedom).

Do all of your work on notebook paper. Label each activity that you complete, using the labels written in large print in each square on the menu. When you complete all three activities in a row, column, or diagonal, you have a Tic-Tac-Toe. You can turn in your paper or you can complete three more activities for another win.

Tic-Tac-Toe Menus

Tic-Tac-Toe Menu 2

Outline Make an outline about all you know about your topic.	**Judge** What is interesting about your topic? What is not interesting?	**Categorize** List all of the groups that your topic belongs to.
Characterize Make a list of your topic's characteristics. What else in the world has similar characteristics to it?	**Prove** Write something true about your topic. Prove that this is true. List evidence to support your proof.	**Summarize** Summarize the most important facts about your topic.
Modify Explain how you could change your topic to make it better.	**Compare** Brainstorm a list of at least 10 things similar to your topic. Star those things that are most like it.	**Blame** What might your topic be blamed for? List at least three things. Explain why it is to blame for all three.

Directions: Choose three activities in a row, column, or diagonal about your topic. The topic may be one your teacher selected, or one you may be asked to choose. It might be an event, an animal, a person, a place, an object, an invention, a story plot, or a concept (such as freedom).

Do all of your work on notebook paper. Label each activity that you complete, using the labels written in large print in each square on the menu. When you complete all three activities in a row, column, or diagonal, you have a Tic-Tac-Toe. You can turn in your paper or you can complete three more activities for another win.

Tic-Tac-Toe Menu 3

Apply It Differently Make up three mathematical word problems related to your topic.	**Explain Its Effects** List at least 10 ways your topic has affected our world.	**Change** Change one thing about your topic. Brainstorm a list of who this change would affect and why.
Classify Put your topic in a subgroup. Name the others members of this subgroup.	**Associate** What things come to your mind when you think about your topic?	**Argue for or Against** Take a stand for or against your topic. Give your reasons why.
Give It a Friend Describe who or what would be a friend of your topic. Explain why the two would be good friends.	**Dissect** List at least 10 of your topic's different parts. Pick two parts and explain their importance to it.	**Give It Gratitude** List at least 10 things, people, or events that would be grateful for your topic. Pick one and explain the reason for the gratitude.

Directions: Choose three activities in a row, column, or diagonal about your topic. The topic may be one your teacher selected, or one you may be asked to choose. It might be an event, an animal, a person, a place, an object, an invention, a story plot, or a concept (such as freedom).

Do all of your work on notebook paper. Label each activity that you complete, using the labels written in large print in each square on the menu. When you complete all three activities in a row, column, or diagonal, you have a Tic-Tac-Toe. You can turn in your paper or you can complete three more activities for another win.

A GUIDE TO DEVELOPING DIFFERENTIATED UNITS FOR TRADE BOOKS AND SHORT STORIES

Using literature and trade books is an excellent way to turn students onto reading. It can be difficult, however, because of the time required to develop questions and activities to accompany the text. Add differentiation to the equation, and the task can be overwhelming.

To develop a unit for a trade book or short story, first list your objectives for the unit. Then, use this guide to identify those questions and activities that will enable your students to meet your objectives. The guide is divided into three sections, covering activities before reading, during reading, and after reading. Each one contains a menu of ideas for questions and activities from which you can choose.

If your whole class is reading the same book, you can differentiate your instruction by varying the questions you ask and by assigning different activities and projects to different groups. You might circle the questions and activities for one group in red, another group in blue, and a third in green. This strategy will enable you to use the same guide for all of your groups.

Before Students Read

Choose one or more of these strategies to introduce a book or story to your students. The activities will motivate them to read and will enhance their understanding of the text.

Book Museum. A book museum is a portable museum that contains objects important in a story or book. The objects might be literal replications of items found in a story, or they might be symbolic. For example, a matchbox would be a literal replication of the bed used by Stuart in the book, *Stuart Little,* and a Valentine heart candy might be placed in the museum to symbolize the friendship between two characters in a story.

The museum provides an interesting introduction to a book. The objects provide excellent clues for making inferences and predictions about the story.

Directions:

1. Make a list of objects that are important to the story. Gather as many of the objects as you can find.
2. Make labels for each object using index cards. Explain on the card why the object was significant. For older or more advanced students, omit the labels.
3. Find a box, old suitcase, or plastic tub and place the objects and labels inside.
4. Ask students to predict why each object might be important to the story. You also may ask students to predict, based on the objects in the museum, what the book or story is about.

Book Talk. A book talk is a brief talk made by the teacher, highlighting some of the important themes, characters, or plot in the book students will read. Students will have a chance to share their predictions and expectations. The talk is given in order to entice students to read the book, but also provides an opportunity for students to share other books that they enjoyed (Thompkins, 1997).

Directions:

1. Select a book or a group of books that you want introduced to the class. A group of books might be on a variety of levels. After the introduction, direct students to select one to read.
2. Display the book(s) for the talk. You might make a poster and advertise the book talk several days prior.
3. During the talk, give brief information about the content, characters, plot, and so on. Read an excerpt.
4. After you have modeled how to lead a book talk, you might want to encourage students to give book talks about books they have read and enjoyed.

Book Walk. A book walk is a figurative "walk," an exploration of a book, its title, author, cover, endorsements, jacket blurb, and table of contents. This strategy will encourage students to think about what they will read by asking questions that focus on a specific aspect of the book and establish a purpose for their reading (see Table 3).

Directions:

1. Choose one or more of the questions listed in Table 3 to explore a book with your students before they begin reading it.

Table 3
Book Walk Questions

Questions Pertaining to . . .	Questions
Title	What does the title suggest about this story? What clues about the book are in this title? What do you predict this book is about?
Author	Have you read other books by this author? What do you know about this author? What have other people said about this author?
Cover Artwork	What does the art suggest about the story? What predictions about the story can you make from examining the picture on the cover? Is there any symbolism in the art on the cover? Discuss.
Endorsements	What do the endorsements suggest to you about the book and the author? How do the endorsements affect you?
Book Jacket Blurb	What predictions about this book can you make from reading the blurb on the book jacket? Does this description of the book make you eager to read it? Why or why not?
Table of Contents	What do the chapter titles suggest to you about the book's plot and/or characters? Which chapter titles sound interesting to you? What chapter titles make you eager to read the book?

2. Discuss their responses in a class or group discussion or ask students to respond individually to the questions in their reading log (see below).

3. To differentiate, vary the questions you ask groups of students based on skill level.

Reading Log. A reading log is simply a journal in which students respond in a variety of ways to the book or story they are reading. It contains a collection of responses, questions, quick writes, quick draws, webs, diagrams, notes, and stories a student has written while reading books and stories throughout the school year (Thompkins, 1997).

Directions:

1. Ask students to designate a spiral notebook to be used as their reading log.

2. Plan activities for students to complete in their logs while reading a trade book or story. Suggestions for reading log activities, including quick-writes and quick-draws, are addressed below.

3. Monitor the log periodically. It provides a guide to how well the students are understanding and interpreting what they are reading. It also might reveal questions that need clarification.

Picture Walk. As the name suggests, a picture walk is a walk through the pictures in a story or book. During the walk, students search each picture for details and clues about the story.

Pictures play an important role in picture books, trade books, and textbooks, and students discuss how the illustrations reflect the text. Exploring the pictures, students learn to search for details, and make inferences and predictions. They might explore the illustrator's style and compare it to other artists. They might discuss how the illustrations enhance the story and evaluate their effectiveness.

Directions:
1. Ask students to examine illustrations on the cover and/or throughout the book. Guide them to look for meaning related to story and for clues that reveal characters, setting, and plot.
2. Ask students to share their ideas in a group discussion or to do a quick-write or quick-draw in their reading logs.

Quick-Write and Quick-Draw. In a quick-write, students jot down ideas, thoughts, and feelings in their reading logs in response to questions, statements, and quotes found in their reading. Children in K–2 might do a quick-draw, sketching their ideas instead of writing about them.

Quick-writing helps students to focus their thinking and can help them organize their thoughts and ideas. It provides the opportunity for students to brainstorm on paper and to respond without the fear of being wrong. It also provides a record of their initial ideas about a book, story, or topic. Later, they can refer back to the quick-write and determine if their thinking or ideas changed after they read a book or a story (Thompkins, 1997).

Directions:
1. Give students a topic or question and allow 5–10 minutes for them to write about it in their reading log. The questions, statements, and quotes might focus on key ideas, make connections between the story and their own personal experiences, or relate the story to others they have read.

Check if you agree or disagree with each statement:

Agree	Disagree	Statement
		People would be happier if they knew that they could live forever.
		Immorality can become claustrophobic.
		The pain of immorality would result from losing loved ones who were not immortal.
		Secrets are burdens.
		Secrets often produce fear.
		Death might become a gift to the immortal.

FIGURE 1. Sample anticipation guide for *Tuck Everlasting* by Natalie Babbit.

    2. Explain that in a quick-write, they need not focus on spelling, punctuation, or grammar.

    3. They can share their quick-writes with a partner or with the class.

    4. After they have shared and listened to the ideas of their classmates, you might ask students to review their own quick-write and underline key ideas. They might write more about the topic, adding new ideas they learned from other students.

Anticipation Guide. An anticipation guide is a list of statements relating to the big ideas or themes found in a particular text. Students are asked to agree or disagree with each statement. It provides a hook to motivate students to read an assigned text by involving them emotionally in its content (Thompkins, 1997). For an example, see Figure 1.

Directions:

    1. When preparing questions or activities, consider the big ideas of the work. List these. Then, write statements relating to each idea.

    2. Print a copy of the statements for each student, or read them aloud.

    3. Ask students to check off whether they agree or disagree with each one.

    4. After reading the text, ask students to compare their opinions with those of the author, based on characters' actions and dialogue, or implied ideas found in narrative.

Connect the Content. Connect the content is a strategy that directs students to connect the text they will read to their personal experience, prior knowledge, or other literature. This strategy provides students with a foundation that will help them make sense of what they read.

Directions:

1. Relate the information regarding characters, setting, or plot revealed in a book talk, book museum, or book/picture walk to the student's personal experience. Ask one or more of these questions and discuss:

   - Does the character described in the blurb on the book jacket remind you of anyone that you know?
   - Have you ever had an experience similar to the one illustrated on the book jacket or described in the blurb?
   - Have you ever been in a situation like the one described in the synopsis on the book jacket?
   - Does the character, setting, or plot remind you of a book or story that you have read before?

2. To differentiate, ask higher level questions:

   - How might you react if you found yourself in the situation described on the book jacket? How do you predict the character will react?
   - Based on the information revealed in the book talk/museum or on the book jacket, what do you think you might learn from reading this book?
   - How does this book jacket compare with that of your favorite book? Show your ideas in a Venn diagram in your reading log.
   - How would you rate the book jacket in terms of enticing you to read the book? Give it a 5 for a job well done, and a 1 for a jacket that didn't motivate you at all to read.

Make Predictions. Students predict what the book or chapter is about, using clues from the title and the pictures and text on the book jacket.

This strategy provides a focus and sets a purpose for reading. As the students read the text, they check to find out if their predictions were correct. If reading a novel, they might consider clues from previous chapters when making predictions.

Directions:

1. Ask students to examine the book jacket, jotting down observations about the characters, setting, and plot.

2. Using this information, ask them to record their predictions in a double-entry journal (see below for description).

To differentiate:
1. Challenge students to defend their predictions by justifying the evidence they used to make them.
2. Challenge students to evaluate their evidence. First, ask them to list all of the evidence they used when making their predictions. Then, evaluate each piece of evidence, using a 3-prong scale, with 3 being the highest rating.

Double-Entry Journal. In a double-entry journal, the page is divided into two columns. Students write their predictions about what will happen in the story in one column and record what actually happens in the other column after they have read the text (Thompkins, 1997).

Double-entry journals can be used in a variety of ways. In addition to providing an opportunity for students to make predictions, they can be used to react to a particular excerpt or quote. Double-entry journals are natural differentiation tools because there is no "right" answer. Ask students to write an excerpt or quote from a book or story they are reading in the left-hand column. Then, have them write their thoughts, ideas, and reactions to the excerpt in the right-hand column. They might relate the excerpt to their own experience, ask a question regarding it, express an opinion about it, or connect it to a topic they have already studied. They might also use the journal to illustrate cause and effect.

Directions:
1. Students fold their paper in half lengthwise, making two columns.
2. In the left-hand column, students list quotes, characters, settings from the books, or they write down notes as they are reading. They should put an appropriate title at the top of the column, such as *Quotes, Characters' Actions, Notes*, and so on.
3. The right-hand column should be titled, *My Reactions*. As the title suggests, the students write their reaction to whatever they listed on the left.

Focus on the Words. This strategy introduces significant words students will encounter in the text they will read. These words can be included in the vocabulary study related to their reading. This strategy will enable students to identify unknown words in the text and to explore their meaning prior to reading.

Directions:
1. List words on the board that you want to include in a vocabulary study after the reading. Briefly discuss their meaning. Ask students to look for these words when they read.
2. In addition, ask students to jot down additional words they find in the text that they can't define or pronounce. Direct them to write the words in their reading log or in a separate vocabulary notebook.

To differentiate:
1. Assign different vocabulary words to different groups based on reading ability.

While Students Read

In order for students to be engaged when reading, they must be active participants in the process and interact with the text. Skilled readers apply a variety of strategies that enable them to become involved with what they're reading.

Examine the list of strategies listed in this section. Consider the text your students will read and select a strategy that is appropriate for that text. Direct your students to focus on the strategy when reading. Encourage them to take notes as they read and record in their reading log. Strategies #4 and #5 are challenging and are appropriate for advanced students.

Set a Purpose for Reading. Select a purpose from Table 4 that is appropriate for the text your students will read. Explain why you want this purpose to be their focus. If indicated in the chart, direct your students to take notes and record in their reading log.

Discuss this strategy with your students. Explore why it is a strategy good readers use to better understand what they're reading. Explain that identifying the purpose helps the reader focus on the text, which leads to better comprehension and understanding.

Table 5 contains a series of focus questions pertaining to characters, setting, and plot.

Table 4
Purpose for Reading

Purpose for Reading	Is Note-Taking Useful? If Yes, Why?
Have fun and read simply for pleasure.	No.
Gather information.	Yes. Students can rely on notes for accuracy rather than memory.
Check predictions.	Yes. Students may continue to check predictions throughout the text and use their notes as a reference point for comparison.
Check and revise initial reactions to characters, their actions, and the plot.	Yes. Students can refer to notes when comparing reactions to various sections of a novel or story.
Answer questions regarding characters, conflicts, plot, and so on. (If you select this purpose, choose questions from the list in Table 5 in order to narrow the focus.)	Yes. Students can refer to notes during class or group discussions and when completing individual assignments regarding the text.
Examine the author's craft. (If you select this purpose, choose questions from the list pertaining to the author's craft on page 27 in order to narrow the focus.)	Yes. Students can refer to notes during class discussion. Notes will reinforce understanding of literary techniques and devices the author used.

Table 5
Questions Focusing on Characters, Setting, and Plot

Question's Focus	Questions
Character traits	What are the physical traits of the major characters? What are the characters' interior traits (personality, emotions, likes/dislikes, abilities)?
Character motivation	Why do the major characters act the way they do?
Characters' points of view	What is the main character's point of view about events that happen? What are the other major characters' points of view about events? Are any of the points of view in conflict?
Characters' interaction	How do the major characters interact when together in the same scene? What does the main character's dialogue reveal about him or her? What does dialogue between two characters reveal about the characters and/or the plot?
Character's problem	What are the major problems the characters face in the story? How did they react to it? How did they solve it?
Setting	What is the story's setting and how does it relate to the plot?
Plot	What is the major conflict in the story? What is the sequence of events that occur in the story? What effects does the conflict cause? What are the main events that follow the conflict?

Make Personal Connections. When students discover similarities between their own lives and experiences and those of the characters they're reading about, they become more emotionally involved in the story.

Ask students to compare and contrast their lives and experiences to the characters, setting, or plot in the story as they read. Direct them to take notes and record these similarities and differences in their reading log.

Visualize. Excellent readers can easily visualize the characters, setting, and action in the story they're reading. Ask students when they read to focus on the visual images the text creates in their mind's "eye." Direct them to jot down the page numbers containing passages that helped them visualize the most detailed pictures in their mind.

Ask Self-Reflective Questions. Advanced readers welcome questions regarding their reactions to the text and their understanding of what they are reading. If you select this strategy, choose one of the questions below in order to help students narrow their focus. Direct students to take notes and record their responses in their reading log.

Questions advanced readers might ask:

- What is the character's motivation for taking a specific action? Do I agree with this? Would I have reacted the same way?
- How did the character react to an event or to the action of another character? Was this reaction valid? Would I react the same way?
- Do I understand this metaphor? What does it mean? Does the metaphor work for me?
- Do I really understand this passage?
- Is there anything in this story that doesn't make sense to me?
- Is there anything in this story that is confusing to me?

Questions focusing on author's craft:

- How does the author reveal emotions in the story?
- How does the author set the mood?
- How does the author build tension in the story?
- What metaphors does the author use?
- What figurative language does the author use?

Apply What I Learned. Advanced readers often evaluate what they read in terms of its usefulness and relevance to their lives. If they determine the text has value, then it is meaningful to them and they become more involved in what they're reading. If you select this strategy, choose one of the questions below in order to narrow the focus. Direct students to take notes and record their responses in their reading log.

Questions the advanced reader might ask when reading in order to determine the value of the text:

- How is this information useful to me?
- How might I use this information?
- What does this story mean to me?
- What life lessons did I learn? How might I apply those lessons in my life?
- What can I learn about myself from reading this text?
- How does this text challenge me to think?

After Students Read

After reading, have your students engage in activities that guide them to think, react, interpret, and evaluate the text. Choose one or more of these activities for your students to complete.

Respond to Focus Question. Ask students to think about the answers they uncovered to their focus question while reading (see Table 5). Using one of the strategies listed below, direct students to show what they learned.

- Discuss the following question in a group or whole-class discussion: (e.g., "What did you learn in this chapter about your character? His motivation? His traits?").
- Check your predictions in your double-entry journal. Compare them to what you read and record your findings in your journal.
- Write the answer to your focus question in your double-entry journal. Also, write your reaction to what you learned (e.g., "Were you surprised by a particular event? Were you surprised by a particular action your character took? Do you agree with this action?").
- List metaphors, interesting use of the language, and unfamiliar words in your double-entry journal. Explain each or react to them, expressing your feelings about the use of language.

- Organize your thinking regarding character, setting, or plot using the Literature Graphic Organizers (see pp 45–58).

React to What Was Read. Ask students how they reacted to what they read and record their responses in their reading log. Choose one or more of these questions for them to answer:
- What did you like about what you read? What didn't you like? Why?
- What was your favorite part of the chapter or story?
- Were there any funny, sad, or exciting parts? Describe them.
- How did you feel about the character? Explain.
- What was something the character did that you liked? Why did you like it?
- What was something the character did that you did not like? Why?
- Describe the sights, sounds, and smells in the chapter or story.

Have a Grand Conversation. A grand conversation (Eeds & Wells, 1989; Peterson & Eeds, 1990) is a formal conversation among a small group of students who discuss their interpretations and explore their feelings about a book. It may be held after every story or after each chapter in a trade book. Grand conversations provide an opportunity for students to have a discussion about a book with their peers, not concerning themselves with the traditional comprehension skills but rather with their feelings, opinions, and ideas about the story, its characters, and plot.

Directions:
1. Students sit in a circle during the grand conversation in order for everyone to see every person participating in the discussion.
2. Students must have read the chapter or story in order to participate.
3. The teacher or a group leader serves as the facilitator. She starts the conversation by simply asking students what they would like to share about the chapter or story.
4. Each student should participate. Because the conversations usually last 10–20 minutes, students should not be allowed to make more than two or three comments until everyone has had an opportunity to talk.

5. After students have shared their initial comments, the teacher might focus the conversation on a particular area, such as illustrations, characters, plot, or themes.

Discussion questions for a grand conversation:

- What did you like about the chapter or story? What didn't you like? Explain your answers.
- What was your favorite part of the chapter or story?
- Describe any funny, sad, or exciting parts.
- What did you learn about the character or plot in this chapter or story?
- Describe the feelings the character had in this chapter or story. Explain why he or she had these feelings.
- What did the character say that was especially important? Explain how this dialogue was important.
- What was one important thing that the character did in this chapter or story? Explain why it was important.
- What problem did the character have? How did he or she address it? Was it successful? Why or why not?
- What caused the character's problem? How might the character have avoided the problem?
- Did the character have any conflicts or doubts in this chapter or story? Describe.
- What new character was introduced in this chapter or story? Describe the character. Why do you think he or she is in the story?
- Who is the villain (antagonist) in the story? What did he or she do that was against the main character? Why do you think he or she did this?
- How did the characters in the chapter or story interact? How did they get along?
- Describe a conversation between any two characters. Why were they having this conversation? How was it related to the overall plot or theme?
- How does the author reveal the passage of time in the story?
- How does the author let you know in what time period the story takes place?

- What was the most important event in this chapter or story? What events led up to this one?
- Why was this chapter or story important?
- How did the author keep you interested in the chapter or story? Explain.
- What do you like about the author's writing? What don't you like? Explain.
- Did the author use flashbacks or foreshadowing in the story? Explain.
- What symbols did the author use in the story?

Digging Deeper With Bloom. Create a worksheet based on Bloom's Revised taxonomy. Select questions from the following list, and ask students to record their responses in their reading log.

To differentiate, make three different worksheets. Select questions for each worksheet appropriate for a specific group of students based on their ability and skill level.

Remembering (Knowledge):
- Identify the characters in the story. Tell how they are related to one another (e.g., sister, friend, mother, and so on).
- What happens to the main character in the chapter or story?
- What is the main character's problem? How does he or she react to this problem? How does he or she solve it?
- Make a facts chart about the events in the story. Answer these questions about the events in your chart. Where? When? Why? Who caused the event? Who was affected by it?
- Make a chart to record the following information about each character in the story: gender, age (e.g., toddler, kid, teenager, adult), and grade or job if an adult.
- List objects used by the characters in the story. Pick three of the objects, and tell how each of these is used.
- List five things you know about the story's setting.
- List all of the places the main character visits in the story.
- What is the climate and/or weather like in the story? Find evidence to support your ideas.

- Draw a map of the setting. Locate the important spots and label them.
- List five things that happened in the story in the order in which they happened.
- Make up a true/false test about the story and include an answer sheet.

Understanding (Comprehension):

- Describe what the main character might see, hear, smell, and touch. List the evidence to support your ideas.
- Quote your main character. Pick one thing that the character said that was important. Write the quote, and explain why this quote is important.
- Draw a cartoon to illustrate a day in the life of one of the main characters.
- Draw a symbol that will help someone better understand the main character.
- Retell the story in your own words. Write your retelling in your reading log.
- What is the main idea in the story?
- Summarize the story.
- How much time passes in the story? How do you know this?
- Make a timeline that illustrates events in the story.
- Make a web, putting the main character's problem in the center. Complete the web, focusing on the "what," "when," "where," "why," and "how" of the problem.
- Develop a poster containing numbers that are related to the story.
- Develop a list of nouns that indicate who the main character is.

Applying (Application):

- If the main character had _____, how many different ways could he or she use it? Choose one and explain how it would be helpful.
- What questions might you ask the main character that would help you understand why he or she did something? List the questions.
- What did you learn in the story that could help you in your day-to-day life? Explain how it might help.

- What could you change in the setting that would help the main character? Explain how it might help.
- Predict how the main character might react if one of the other characters was taken out of the story. Explain who was eliminated and give reasons for your prediction.
- Predict what might happen to the character in the future, after the story's ending. Explain your prediction.
- How many different ways might you group the characters in the story? List the characters in each group and give each group a title.
- What if you were added to the story? How might you change it?
- Could this story have taken place in a different time period? Explain your answer. If it could, how might the different time affect the story?
- What if the setting in the story was changed to a different locale with a different climate, different surroundings, and so on—how might this change the story?
- Is there another solution to the character's problem other than the one described in the story? Describe this alternative solution.
- Based on what you know about the main character, what problem might the character have other than the ones dealt with in the story? Explain why you think the character could have this problem.

Analyzing (Analysis):
- Categorize all the facts you know about the main character. Put this data into a chart.
- List three events that occurred in the main character's life. Pick one. What would have changed in the character's life if this event had not happened? Explain and give evidence to support your ideas.
- How are you like the main character? How are you different? Make a Venn diagram to illustrate the data.
- How is the setting in the story like the setting in your own life? How is it different? List as many similarities and differences as you can.
- Which event did the main character like best in the story? Describe the event and explain why you think this is the character's favorite.
- What might be the main character's greatest fear? Why? Explain.
- What might make the main character angry? Why? Explain.

- What secret might the main character have? Describe the secret and why the main character might have it.
- Compare and contrast the personality of the significant characters in your story. Show the comparison in a Venn diagram.
- What patterns can you find in the main character's behavior? Describe the patterns.
- How do the other characters feel about the main character? What evidence do you have for thinking this? Make a chart and record how each character feels and the evidence you found in the story that substantiates your idea.

Evaluating (Evaluation):
- List five descriptive words you found in the story. Put a #1 by the most descriptive word, a #2 by the second most, and so on.
- What did you like best about the story? Why? What did you like the least? Explain.
- What is the main character's very best quality? Why do you think so? What is the worst quality? Explain.
- What trait does the main character have that is most valuable to his or her survival? Explain. What characteristic is most valuable to his or her happiness? Explain.
- Prioritize the major events in the chapter or story in terms of their significance in the story's plot, listing the most significant one first.
- What event in the story most affected the main character? Explain and find evidence to support your answer.
- What other character most affected the main character? Explain and find evidence to support your answer.
- Who was your favorite character in the story? Explain your reasons.
- What is the best aspect of the setting? Explain. What is the worst? Explain.
- What criteria would you use to judge the main character's actions? Explain.
- List criteria you might use to evaluate how the character solved a problem in the story. Rate the criteria, putting #1 beside the best.
- Choose an action that the main character took in the story. Judge for or against this action and give the reasons and evidence to support your judgment.

Creating (Synthesis):

- Write an epilogue to the chapter, book, or story.
- Write a prologue to the chapter, book, or story.
- Draw a cartoon adventure that the main character might have based on the facts you learned about him or her.
- Design a new object that could be used by the main character instead of one that he or she used. Explain how this might be more useful.
- Design an invention that would protect the main character from a problem he or she was having in the story. Explain how it would provide protection.
- What might a character in the story do to improve him- or herself? Explain your answer.
- How might you improve the setting for the character? Draw a picture with the character in the changed setting.
- List the personality traits of two characters in the story. Combine some of the traits from one list with some from the other to create a new character. Name the character and describe him or her. If this character was placed in the story, how might he or she change it?
- How would the story be different if the main character were like you? How would it stay the same? Explain.
- Change one of the events in the story. How would this change affect the story's ending? Explain.
- Add an event to the story. Describe this event and explain how it would affect the story.
- Rearrange the characters in the story, making a minor character the main one. How would this rearrangement affect the story? Explain your answer.

Make Personal Connections. Ask students how the story or book relates to their own lives. Choose one or more of the questions below to discuss in a group or whole-class setting. Or, ask students to record their responses in their reading log.

- How are you and the main character are alike/different? Show in a Venn diagram in your reading journal.
- Which character is most like you? Explain the similarities.
- Which character is very different from you? Explain the differences.
- In what ways is the setting like your home and town? Different?

■ Have you ever had an experience like one the character had in the chapter or story? Explain your ideas in your reading journal.

Connect to Other Literature. Ask students how the story or book relates to other books they have read. Choose one or more of the questions below to discuss in a group or whole-class setting. Or, ask students to record their responses in their reading log.

■ Is there a character in another story you have read that is similar to this one? How are they alike? How are they different? Illustrate these ideas in a Venn diagram in your reading journal.

■ Have you read another story that has a plot similar to this one? Explain in your reading journal how the two stories are similar.

Explore the Author's Craft. Ask students to reread sections of the text in order to examine the author's craft. Choose one or more of the questions below to discuss in a group or whole-class setting. Or, ask students to record their responses in their reading log.

■ What special words did the author use to help you see things in the story, hear things in the story, and smell things in the story?

■ How did the author describe the character so you could picture what he or she looked like in your mind? List words, phrases, sentences, or similes the author used to help paint the picture.

■ How did the author keep you interested in the story? Explain.

■ How effective was the author in creating tension in the story?

Reread to Explore Memorable Quotes. Ask students to reread a section of the story or book to find memorable quotes: those sayings, expressions, phrases, sentences, metaphors, or similes that seemed to jump off the page. Direct them to use their double-entry journal in their reading log. List the quotes in the left-hand column. Ask them to tell why they liked the quote or how it made them feel in the right-hand column.

Reread to Explore Vocabulary Words. Ask students to reread the text in order to identify vocabulary words. Choose one or more of these tasks and ask students to record their responses in their reading log.

■ List unfamiliar words that you found in the chapter or story. Suggest these for our word wall (see explanation below).

- Complete a Vocabulary Graphic Organizer (see pp. 59–64) to explore the assigned words for vocabulary study or complete one or more activities listed in the vocabulary study (see pp. 41–44).
- A word wall is a poster on which words from a particular story are written. These words usually are those that are key to the story and/or those that are unfamiliar in meaning or spelling to the student (Thompkins, 1997). By displaying the word wall in the class, students are exposed to the words on a daily basis. The words, therefore, are more likely to bc used in their writing and the students are more likely to learn their spelling and meaning.

Directions for creating a word wall:
- While reading, students list unfamiliar words in their reading logs and those that are difficult to pronounce or spell. They also might include on their list those words that are key words in the story.
- Students read the words on their list and the teacher records them on a poster or on butcher paper.
- The teacher might designate certain words for vocabulary study, or for a spelling list.
- The word wall is displayed in the room. Students may refer to it for correct spelling and they might review for vocabulary study.

Evaluate the Book, Chapter, or Story You Have Read. Ask students to evaluate what they read. Choose one or more of the questions below to discuss in a group or whole-class setting. Or, ask students to record their responses in their reading log.
- What did you like about the book? Why did you like it?
- What didn't you like? Why?
- How might the book, chapter, or story be improved?
- Did you like the characters in the story? Why or why not?
- What did you like about the author's writing? What didn't you like?
- Would you recommend this book? Why or why not?
- Who do you know who would really like this book? Why would he or she like it?

Produce a Product About the Story or Book. Ask students to produce a product related to the story or book they read. Choose a project from the Book Projects list below. Evaluate the project, using a rubric. Discuss the criteria on the rubric with students when giving the assignment. (See Chapter 6 for rubric examples.)

BOOK PROJECTS

Projects Students Write

- Create an alphabet book using words that were important to the book's characters, setting, and plot.
- Retell the story for a picture book. Write and illustrate this new abbreviated version.
- Write a sequel to the book.
- Write an epilogue for the book. Title it "Ten Years Later."
- Think about what might have been happening one year before the story in the book took place. Describe these events in a prologue to the book.
- Rewrite the ending of the story.
- Rewrite the story in a different time period.
- Rewrite the story in a different setting.
- Rewrite the story by having the character solve the problem in a different way.
- Put yourself in the story as one of the main characters. Rewrite the story with this additional character.
- Take an important character out of the book. Rewrite the story without this character.
- Write a paragraph describing your favorite character.
- Write a letter to your favorite character, explaining why you would like him or her as a friend.
- You are pen pals with the main character. Write a letter that he or she might send you, describing the things happening in his or her life. Answer the letter, telling about your own life.
- Write a descriptive paragraph of the villain in the story.

- Write a list of questions you would like to ask the villain in the story. Based on what you learned about the villain, how do you think he or she might answer your questions?
- Retell the story from the villain's point of view.
- Rewrite the book as a radio play with sound effects and music.
- Pretend to be the main character and write your autobiography.
- Write a newspaper, using headlines to tell about the important events in the book. Include other information about the book in ads, pictures, a weather report, and so on.
- Write a series of letters that two of the characters write to each other discussing their adventures in the book.
- Write a poem related to the book.
- Make up mathematical word problems relating to your book or story and ask your friends to solve them. Make sure you have an answer key for them to check their answers.
- Write one or more matrix logic puzzles relating to your book.
- Write a persuasive paragraph explaining why students should or should not have to read this book in school.
- Write a letter to the book's editor explaining how the book might be improved.
- Write a letter to Steven Spielberg in which you try to convince him to make a movie about the book.
- Write a list of criteria an editor might use to evaluate the illustrations on the cover of this book. Make up standards to accompany the criteria. Use these criteria and standards to evaluate the cover.

Projects Students Build or Design

- Decorate a cereal box like a book jacket. Include a synopsis on the jacket.
- Make a "Who Said It?" box. Decorate a box (e.g., cereal or shoe box, coffee can) with colorful speech balloons. Include the name of the book, the author, and the title "Who Said It?" in the decorations. Pick quotes from the book, and write these quotes on large speech balloons made out of note cards—one quote per balloon. Do not write the name of the character who said the quote. Ask classmates

to pull the balloons from the box, read the quotes, and tell who said each one.

- Find your favorite quotes from the book and design a poster about them.
- Make a book bag using a paper sack. Decorate the bag, putting artifacts inside the bag that tell about the story.
- Construct a mobile of book characters, setting, and/or plot.
- Compile a scrapbook that might have belonged to the main character.
- Construct a flip chart depicting scenes from the book.
- Make a model stage set of the book using a shoebox.
- Make an illustrated timeline of important events in the book.
- Make a collage to illustrate the character, setting, plot, and theme of the book.
- Make a relief map of the setting of the book. Put 3-D models on the map to represent the major landmarks in the story.
- Make a collection of props that might be used if the book was to be produced as a play. Explain the importance of the props on a card attached to each one.
- Design a full-page magazine ad for the book.
- Design a poster, using only nouns, to describe the main character.
- Design a poster, using only verbs, to describe the villain.
- Design a PowerPoint presentation about the book.
- Examine the techniques used by artists when they illustrate a book (e.g., collage, water color, cut-outs, photographs, line drawings, and so on). Make a series of illustrations for the book, using one of these techniques.
- Design a survey a publisher might use to determine if this book would be a bestseller. Ask your friends to complete the survey, and compile the results and report to the class.
- Design an illustrated dictionary of vocabulary words from the book.
- Think about your character in terms of colors that symbolize who he or she is, and use all of these colors in a collage. Have a key that explains why you selected each color.

Projects Students Perform

- Dress up as the character and have someone take photos of you acting out events in the story. Arrange the photos on a poster in order.
- Dress up as the character and think about the problems you faced in the story, what caused them, and how you solved them. Tell all in an oral presentation.
- Write a play about the book. Present it using classmates as characters in your play.
- Write a TV commercial advertising the book. Present the commercial to the class.
- Dress up as the villain in your story. Explain yourself and your actions in a monologue.

TIERED ACTIVITIES FOR VOCABULARY STUDY

Vocabulary development is an important component of all units of study in the classroom. No matter the discipline, it is essential that students learn the language associated with a topic they are studying in order to fully understand what they are learning.

This tool provides three lists of activities designed for vocabulary study. The lists are tiered, with Tier A being the least difficult and Tier C the most challenging. The activities can be used for daily practice or homework assignments. Choose one or more of them from the tier that is most appropriate for each specific group of students.

Rather than have all of your students look up every word on the vocabulary list, you might try a jigsaw approach: Hand out the vocabulary list (or write it on the board), and ask students to number the words on the list. Give each student (or pairs of students) a number that corresponds to the words on the list. Explain that they will become experts on the word that matches their number (i.e., student # 1 will become an expert on word #1). Ask students to analyze their word, using the Analysis of a Word graphic organizer (see p. 59).

After completing the graphic organizer, ask students to present their analysis to the class. Their presentation must include *all* of the information on the graphic organizer. They can communicate this information in a variety of ways, including posters, illustrations, computer printouts, and so on.

Direct the other students to take notes during each expert's presentation, jotting down word meanings, parts of speech, and so on. After the presentations, all of the students will have the analysis of all of the words and will be ready to complete any of the tiered vocabulary activities.

Tiered Vocabulary Activities

Tier A (Least Difficult)

1. *Make Flash Cards*: Print words on index cards (one word per card) and write the definition on the back. Ask a friend to hold up the cards one at a time, exposing the word. You give the definition.
2. *Group the Words*: Group the words according to parts of speech or origin.
3. *Alphabetize the Words*: Put the words in alphabetical order.
4. *Words in Print*: Find the words in print from any source and cut out the words. Make a poster, displaying all of the words that you cut out, or write the reference of the source on the poster, including name of source and page number.
5. *Thesaurus Race*: Which word on the vocabulary list has the most words listed in the thesaurus? Look up your word in the thesaurus and list the words found there on a master synonym list.
6. *Write the Word*: Write each of the words in a sentence that illustrates the word's meaning.
7. *Illustrate the Word*: Draw pictures that illustrate the meaning of selected words.
8. *Prefixes and Suffixes*: List the prefixes and suffixes found in the words on the vocabulary list. Find the meaning of each prefix and suffix and make a prefix/suffix dictionary.
9. *What Word Am I?*: Use the What Word Am I? graphic organizer as a guide to write a riddle for the word (see p. 60).

Tier B (Moderately Difficult)

1. *Word Concentration*: Make flash cards by printing words on index cards (one word per card). Write the definition on another set of cards

(one definition per card). Lay the cards face down on a desk. Turn up two at a time and collect matches of words and their definitions.

2. *Synonym Concentration*: Make flash cards by printing words on index cards. Write one synonym for each word on another set of cards. Play concentration, matching words with their synonyms.

3. *Group the Words*: Group the words according to their meaning.

4. *Compare/Contrast*: Compare and contrast two words from the vocabulary list, using a Venn diagram.

5. *Words and Me*: Select words that apply to your own life in any way. List the words and describe how the words apply. Use a graphic organizer to make a chart of your ideas.

6. *Words and Symbols*: Create symbols that illustrate word meaning and explain why the symbol works.

7. *Crazy Sentences*: Write a sentence using as many of the words from the list as you can. The sentences can be crazy but they have to make sense.

8. *Word Mural*: Draw a mural using the illustrations of as many words from the vocabulary list as you can place in your drawing. Each word's illustration must reveal its meaning.

9. *Wanted*: Make a "wanted" poster for a word, using the graphic organizer on page 62.

Tier C (Most Difficult)

1. *Grouping the Words*: How many different ways can you group these words? Name each group.

2. *Word Relationships*: Write the words on index cards (one word per card). Think about how one word might relate to another. One word might lead to another (e.g., *scarcity* might lead to *famine*). Use arrows (→) to indicate this relationship (e.g., *scarcity* → *famine*). One word might be the opposite of another. This relationship can be illustrated using the not equal (≠) sign.

3. *Analogies*: Make up analogies using words (e.g., hot: cold as up: down).

4. *Subtopics*: Select your favorite word. Make a web with this word as one of the subtopics.

5. *Word Rank*: Select your five favorite words. Rank them from your *most favorite* (1) to *least favorite* (5) in the group of five. Defend your first choice, giving reasons why it is your favorite.

6. *Make Up a Game*: Make up a game using flash cards of all of the vocabulary words.

7. *Write a Story*: Write a story using all of the words from the vocabulary list.

8. *Coat of Arms*: Choose four words from the list that are related. Draw a coat of arms, a shield divided into four sections. Draw a symbol for one word in the first section. The symbol should reflect the word's meaning. Draw symbols for the other three words in the other sections. Name this coat of arms.

9. *Should We Keep This Word?* Decide if one of the vocabulary words is useful or not. Use the graphic organizer as a guide for your thinking (see p. 64).

An Analysis of Character Action

Directions: Choose a character from your chapter or story and analyze one thing that character did. Use the graphic organizer to help you with your thinking.

Describe something the character did.

What did the character say or think about it?

How did character feel about it?

Why did the character do it?

Differentiation Made Simple © Prufrock Press • This page may be photocopied or reproduced with permission for classroom use.

Literature Graphic Organizers

Character Attributes

Directions: Choose a character from your chapter or story. Fill in the graphic organizer to describe the character.

Character's Appearance

Character's Feelings

Character's Thoughts

Character's Behavior

Character's Fears

Character's Prized Possessions

Interaction of Two Characters

Directions: Make a list of the main character's actions in the column on the left. Then, list in the right-hand column how another character in the story reacted to each action.

Main Character: _____	Another Character: _____
Actions	**Reactions**

Literature Graphic Organizers

Character Dialogue

Directions: Think of four characters in the chapter or story. Write their names in the rectangles. In the circle, write something the character said. On the back of this page, list each character's name. Beside each name, write a sentence explaining what this dialogue explains about the plot or characters' relationship to each other.

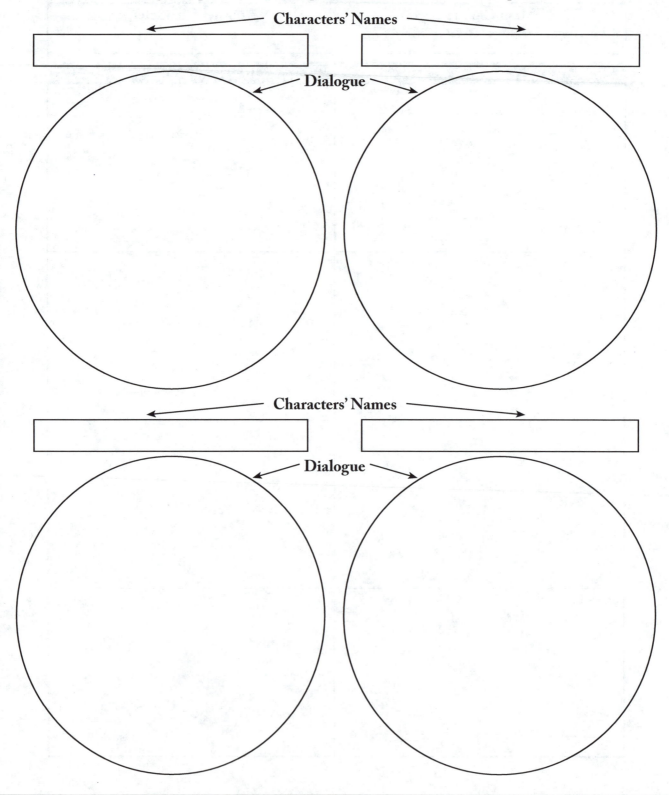

Literature Graphic Organizers

Cause and Effect

Directions: Think about things that happened in the chapter or story. Write these actions in the ovals and what happened as a result of these actions in the rectangles.

Differentiation Made Simple © Prufrock Press • This page may be photocopied or reproduced with permission for classroom use.

Literature Graphic Organizers

Description of Setting

Directions: Choose your favorite setting in the chapter or story. Draw it in the large rectangle. Write a description of it in the space below. Put as many details as you can in both your drawing and your description.

_____

_____

_____

_____

_____

_____

_____

Story Map

Directions: Make a "map" of the story by completing this organizer.

Title:

Setting:

Main
Characters

Problem or Conflict

Events

Solution

Literature Graphic Organizers

Conflict Map

Directions: Use the graphic organizer to map out the conflict in the plot of the chapter or story.

Character's Problem	More Details About Problem

Resolution	More Details About Resolution

Name: _____   Date: _____

Compare/Contrast

Directions: Choose two characters from the chapter or story. Put the name of the
first character in the rectangle labeled, "1." Put the second character's name in the
oval labeled, "2." Then complete the chart, listing traits or characteristics of each
in the appropriate shape.

Characters to Be Compared

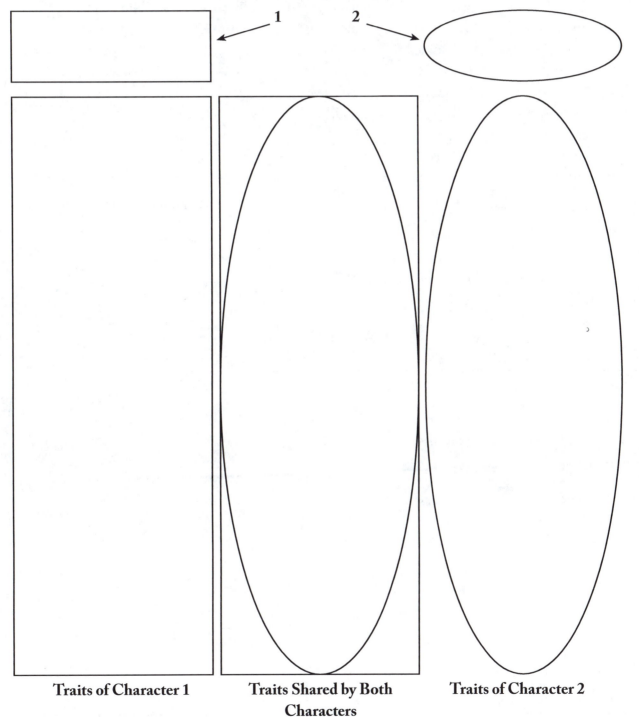

Traits of Character 1   **Traits Shared by Both**   **Traits of Character 2**
                                   Characters

Literature Graphic Organizers

Character Study

Directions: Choose a character in the chapter or story. Think about how this character looks. List these physical traits in the space to the left. In the oval, list the inside character traits (those that describe attitude and feelings). You may choose from some examples listed below or come up with your own.

absentminded	conscientious	frustrated	lively	realistic
aggressive	cooperative	happy-go-	self-assured	resourceful
aloof	critical	lucky	self-reliant	rude
anxious	cynical	humorous	sensitive	stubborn
arrogant	determined	idealistic	serious	talkative
bashful	disgusted	imaginative	shrewd	tenderhearted
bored	disappointed	impulsive	shy	trusting
careless	dull	intelligent	sly	
cautious	easygoing	kind	passive	
confident	envious	lazy	precise	

Physical Traits   **Character Traits**

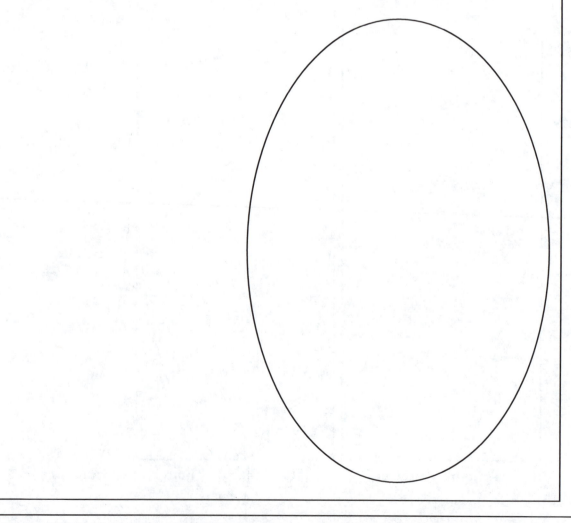

Differentiation Made Simple © Prufrock Press • This page may be photocopied or reproduced with permission for classroom use.

Characters' Points of View (POV)

Directions: Choose an event in the chapter or story. Write the name or short description of this event on the line at the top that reads, "Characters' Points of View About . . ." Think about how the main character (protagonist), the villain (antagonist), and one other character in the story felt about the event. In the appropriate box, write what each character said, thought, or felt about the event you chose. To the right, describe what in the story led you to each conclusion.

Characters' Points of View About . . .	
Main character's POV	**How do you know?**
Villain's POV	**How do you know?**
Another character's POV	**How do you know?**

Literature Graphic Organizers

Chain of Events

Directions: Fill out the organizer, listing events in the chapter or story in the order in which they happened.

This happened:

Then this happened:

Then this:

And this:

Finally, this:

Literature Graphic Organizers

Who Am I?

Directions: Choose a character in the chapter or story. Think of clues that tell something about the character without saying exactly who he or she is. List the clues on the page. See if a friend can identify the character using your clues.

Clue 1:

Clue 2:

Clue 3:

Clue 4:

Clue 5:

Who Am I?

Take It Out

Directions: Think about the major events in the chapter or story. Choose one to eliminate from the story and describe this event in the oval. In the rectangles, write three things that might happen as a result of this event being eliminated.

Describe the Event to Be Eliminated

Describe Three Things That Might Happen Because of This

Analysis of a Word

Directions: Write a word on the top line. Use the organizer to help you analyze the word.

Word: _____

Definition:
Sentence Using Word:

Origin:	Part of Speech:
Synonyms:	**Antonyms:**
Prefixes:	**Suffixes:**

What Word Am I?

Directions: Choose a word and write a riddle about it in the first box. Give clues but don't give the word away. Ask a friend to identify the word, using your clues.

Riddle:

Clue 1:

Clue 2:

Clue 3:

Clue 4:

Clue 5:

What Word Am I?

Words and Me

Directions: Think of four vocabulary words or words in your chapter or story. Write them in the column on the left. Think how each word is like you and describe this similarity in the second column.

Words	This Word Is Like Me Because

Vocabulary Graphic Organizers

Wanted Poster

Directions: Choose a vocabulary word or an important word in your chapter or story. Write the name of the word in the top rectangle. Draw a picture illustrating the word in the large square and explain why the word is wanted in the lower rectangle. Your reason must reflect the word's meaning.

Differentiation Made Simple © Prufrock Press • This page may be photocopied or reproduced with permission for classroom use.

Subtopic

Directions: Choose a vocabulary word or word in your chapter or story. Write the word in the lower right-hand circle. If this word is the subtopic, what is the topic? Write the topic in the center oval. Name three other subtopics. Write these in the other three circles.

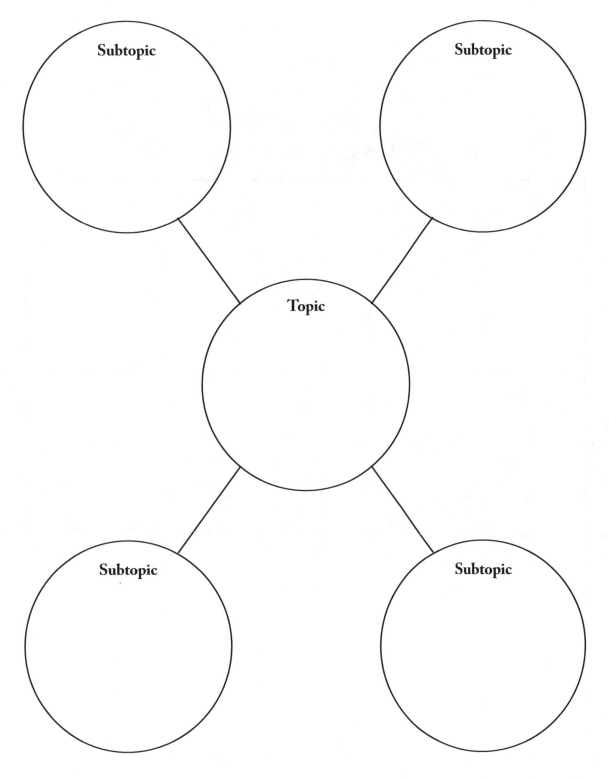

Vocabulary Graphic Organizers

Should We Keep This Word?

Directions: Choose a vocabulary word or word from your chapter or story. Should we keep this word in the English language? You be the judge! Then, list three good reasons why we should or should not keep this word.

Word: _____

Should we keep this word in the English language?

YES   NO

Below, list three good reasons to support your decision.

CHAPTER 4

LEARNING CENTER TASK CARDS

LEARNING centers are specified places in a classroom where individuals or small groups might complete one or more tasks. They are as varied as the teachers who develop them and are used in many different ways. A center might provide opportunities for students to:

- reinforce skills—to practice and apply what they have learned in class;
- examine a topic in more depth than what is covered in the text to encourage students to step beyond the worksheets and tests that usually accompany a chapter in their science, language arts, or social studies book;
- complete fun activities that complement the text or unit;
- research a particular aspect of a concept taught in the text or unit; and
- explore a topic not covered in text or unit. It might be indirectly related to content taught in the class (e.g., if the class is studying the oceans, there might be a center focused on sea life).

Although learning centers can be different in both their focus and their approach, *all* of them should include tasks that address varying levels of difficulty. In doing this, centers provide an effective strategy for differentiation.

The problem with centers is that they require time to create. The task cards in this chapter help alleviate this problem in that they will save you time. The tasks are generic and can be copied and used again and again with a variety of topics.

The Generic Task Cards for a Differentiated Learning Center (pp. 70–99), based on Bloom's Revised taxonomy, can be used with topics you're studying in social studies or science. The Creative Writing Task Cards (pp. 100–109) can be used to make a permanent writing center.

Generic Task Cards for a Differentiated Learning Center

Follow these simple directions to quickly set up a differentiated learning center for all of the units or chapters in the text that you teach in social studies or science.

1. When you are teaching a unit, think about the topic as you read through the task cards. Copy the cards that you want to use. Then, write the name of the topic in the space provided on each card.

2. Cut out the cards and laminate them or put each one in a sandwich bag.

3. Get six envelopes. Copy and cut out the labels on page 69. The labels identify the different levels of Bloom's Revised taxonomy: *Remembering, Understanding, Applying, Analyzing, Evaluating,* and *Creating.* Glue each one onto an envelope.

4. Glue the envelopes on a poster board or tri-fold board. Or, designate a place on a bulletin board for this center. Make a title for the center and attach it to the board. Examples of titles might be "Thinking About Sea Life" or "Thinking About Explorers."

5. Using the labels on the task cards as a guide, put each card into the appropriate envelope.

6. Your center is now ready to use.

7. After you have completed this unit, store the task cards in a file and save it until next year.

Creative Writing Learning Center Guide

In order for students to become good writers, they need to have the opportunity to write—and write often. With all of the content you are required to teach, however, it often is difficult to find time for creative writing in your classroom.

A creative writing learning center can be the answer to this dilemma. It also can provide a strategy for differentiation. If the activities are open-ended or reflect varying levels of difficulty, students can work at their own level of proficiency.

Like all learning centers, a creative writing center requires time to develop. The task cards in this chapter will save you time. They are ready to copy and use. Once copied and put in a center, they can be permanent fixtures in your classroom and used again and again, even by the same students. First, you need to gather and organize materials to help spark students' creativity.

Follow these directions to set up your creative writing learning center.

1. Get six different folders or envelopes large enough to hold 8 x 10-inch pictures and label each one in large letters. Use the following labels:
   - Single Character Folder,
   - Multiple Characters Folder,
   - Setting Folder,
   - Event Folder,
   - Vehicle Folder, and
   - Editing Guide.

2. Cut out pictures from magazines, newspapers, or calendars. *National Geographic* is one of the best sources for these pictures. Find as many pictures as you can that contain the following:
   - one person alone in picture (to be placed in Single Character Folder);
   - multiple people in picture (for Multiple Characters Folder);
   - pictures of scenes without people in the picture (for Setting Folder);
   - pictures of events, such as parades, fairs, sporting games, and performances (for Event Folder); and
   - pictures of vehicles, preferably without people in the pictures (for Vehicle Folder).

3. Put the pictures in sheet protectors and place them in the appropriate envelopes.
4. Make a copy of the Creative Writing Task Cards (see pp. 100–109). Cut out and laminate or put in sheet protectors or sandwich bags.

5. Make several copies of the Student Editing Guide handout (see p. 110). Put the copies in sheet protectors and put in the Editing Guide Folder.

6. Get a box for the center and put all of these items in the box. Label the box "Creative Writing Center" and put the items on a shelf in a corner or on a table designated specifically for this center.

7. After you have prepared everything you need for the center, introduce it to the class. Provide a place in your room where student work from the center can be displayed.

8. Although regular writing activities are encouraged, how often students will write is at your discretion. You do not have to grade every story written by the students. Instead, ask students to select their best story for you to grade (one or two per grading period).

9. All writers need editors. What works best for students is a combination of teacher feedback, peer editing, and self-editing. Encouraging students to edit their own work, even those stories that will not be graded, will not only help improve their own writing, but will make them better editors for their classmates. The Student Editing Guide on page 110 offers basic guidelines for students to follow.

Bloom's Revised Taxonomy Labels

Copy and cut out the labels below and glue each onto an envelope.
These envelopes will hold the task cards for your Differentiated Learning
Center.

REMEMBERING

UNDERSTANDING

APPLYING

ANALYZING

EVALUATING

CREATING

Learning Center Task Cards

Remembering

Create an illustrated history of _____ words.

Remembering

Collect a group of words that relate to _____. Write a definition for each one. Make an exhibit for your collection of words and definitions. Use magic markers, index cards, a cardboard box, and poster board to make your exhibit.

Remembering

Make a true/false test about _____.
Write the answers on a separate sheet of paper.

Remembering

Answer the following questions about
_____: Who? What? Where? When?
Why? How? Using index cards, write each question on one
side and the answers on the other. Quiz your friends to
see if they know the answers.

Remembering

Draw a diagram of _____. Label all of its parts.

Remembering

You were witness to _____. Describe what you saw.

Remembering

Collect 10 pictures of _____. Put them in a book and write captions describing each picture.

Remembering

Make a timeline illustrating events or cycles related to _____.

Remembering

Make an alphabet book about _____.
List one fact that represents each letter on its own page.

Remembering

Collect pictures of _____. Make a
collage using these pictures.

Understanding

Make a timeline to show how _____
has changed over time.

Understanding

List five things that happened to _____.
Why did these things happen? Show your ideas in a two-
column cause/effect chart.

Understanding

Pretend you are _____. Write an
entry in your diary, describing all of the things you did
today.

Understanding

Draw a picture that symbolizes _____.
Explain the symbol on the back of your drawing.

Understanding

Make a web with _____ in the center.

Understanding

How would you summarize what happened when
_____? Write your summary and
make a sketch to illustrate it.

Understanding

How is _____ like
_____? How are they different? Show
your ideas in a Venn diagram.

Understanding

Make a list of facts you know about _____.
Organize this information and put it in a chart.

Differentiation Made Simple © Prufrock Press • This page may be photocopied or reproduced with permission for classroom use.

Understanding

Make a flow chart to illustrate the sequence of events in

_____.

Understanding

Make a "how-to" booklet that relates to

_____. Illustrate each step.

Applying

Make a model to demonstrate how _____ will work. The model can be either a drawing on paper, a three-dimensional model, or one designed on the computer.

Applying

Make a diorama to illustrate an important event related to _____.

Applying

What questions would you ask _____
in an interview? Based on what you know about
_____, how would he or she answer?

Applying

What props would you use if you were putting on a play
about _____? Draw a picture of the
stage set for the play and include each of the props in your
drawing. On the back of your drawing, explain why you are
using each prop.

Applying

Categorize all the facts you know about
_____. Name each category and list
the facts that belong in each one. Put this data into a bar,
line, or pie graph.

Applying

Predict what might happen if _____.
Explain your ideas and give evidence to support the
reasoning behind your prediction.

Applying

Draw a map related to _____. Identify key locations.

Applying

Make up a lesson to teach _____ to second graders. Write your lesson plan, telling what you would do, what materials you would need, and how you would test that the students learned the material.

Applying

Make a poster about _____, using only numbers. On the back of the poster, explain how each number relates to the topic.

Applying

If you ruled the world and could change _____, how would you change it? Illustrate your ideas in a *before* and *after* drawing. Write a caption below each drawing that explains why you made the change and how it affected _____.

Analyzing

How many different groups could _____ belong to? List as many groups as you can and describe what this teaches you in a paragraph, web, or poster.

Analyzing

Break down _____ into all of its many parts. List the parts and explain which part you think is most essential.

Analyzing

How would the world be different if there were no
_____? Make a list of all the positive
changes and negative changes. Then, make a chart or graph
that shows whether these changes would be mostly good
or mostly bad.

Analyzing

How is _____ like you? Make a
diagram containing what you have in common.

Differentiation Made Simple © Prufrock Press • This page may be photocopied or reproduced with permission for classroom use.

Analyzing

Develop a survey related to _____.
Determine the purpose of the survey (what you hope to
learn). Who would you ask to complete it? What questions
would you ask?

Analyzing

What are the essential facts that everyone should know
about _____ in order to understand
it? List these in the first column of a two-column chart. In
the second column, list the facts that might be interesting
but are not necessary for understanding.

Analyzing

What is the relationship between _____ and _____? Illustrate this relationship, using a "family tree" format or web.

Analyzing

Create a "help wanted" advertisement for a job related to _____. Include a job description and a list of qualifications the applicant would need in order to be hired.

Analyzing

List two people who are affected by _____ in some way. Explain each person's point of view regarding _____. Illustrate these two points of view in letters written from one person to the other.

Analyzing

Personify an inanimate (nonliving) object that is related to _____. What is this object's point of view about _____? Write a conversation it might have with its best friend in which it explains its point of view.

Evaluating

What changes do you think _____
should make? Explain why these changes would be good.
Illustrate the changes in a drawing.

Evaluating

_____ is on trial for
_____. Be the defense attorney and
make an argument for why he, she, or it should not be
convicted.

Evaluating

Argue for or against _____. Write a
persuasive argument stating your case, explaining at least
three reasons for your argument.

Evaluating

What are the five most interesting things you learned
about _____? Create a brochure
about _____, using these five things to
encourage people to learn about it.

Evaluating

Would you rather be _____ or
_____? Explain why in at least two
paragraphs.

Evaluating

Create an award that _____ should
receive. List the criteria you used to determine how
_____ was worthy of the award. Make
a certificate or ribbon for the award.

Evaluating

What does _____ have that is most valuable to its survival? Explain why this is so valuable.

Evaluating

What criteria would you use to judge _____? Make a report card for _____ and give it a grade, using these criteria.

Evaluating

What job might you recommend for
_____? Write a letter of
recommendation, including the reason for your
recommendation and evidence to support your reasons.

Evaluating

If you could eliminate one thing from
_____, what would it be? Why would
you choose this to eliminate? How would this elimination
affect _____? How might it affect the
world? Explain your answers in an editorial cartoon.

Creating

Create a code related to _____. See if your friends can "crack" your code.

Creating

Design an invention that would help _____ do _____.

Creating

Think of something _____ might do in order to improve him-, her-, or itself. Explain why this would be an improvement.

Creating

Combine _____ with _____. Name this new object and show how it might be used, by creating an advertisement for this new invention.

Creating

Write lyrics to a song about _____.
Design a CD cover for the song that will let people know what it's about.

Creating

Write a poem, short story, or essay reflecting your thoughts or feelings about _____.

Creating

Think about how things might be in the future. Predict what might happen to _____ in 1,000 years. Give reasons for your prediction and evidence to support it. Illustrate your ideas in a comic strip, or write a science fiction story about it.

Creating

Create a short skit or play about _____. Select cast members from among your classmates, and figure out costumes and the props you will need. Rehearse the skit and perform it for the class.

Creating

Design an advertisement for _____
that would make everyone want to own it.

Creating

Imagine time before _____ and after
_____. What was life like in each of
those time periods? Illustrate your ideas in a timeline or
mural.

Create a Character

Pick a character from the Single Character Folder. Brainstorm some ideas about this character and provide the following details you make up about this character:

- name
- age
- place where character lives
- job (put grade if a student)
- favorite things character does for fun
- favorite people in character's life
- character's enemy (the antagonist)
- talent/ability for which character is proud
- greatest desire
- greatest fear
- greatest problem
- solution to the character's problem (using his or her abilities/talents)

Use this information to write a story about your character.

Super Powers

Pick a character from the Single Character Folder. What if the character had a super power? What is the power? How might this power be used to solve a problem? Write a story about this character with super powers and how he or she solved a critical problem.

Character Traits

Pick a character from the Single Character Folder. What character traits might this character have? Choose at least three. Write a story in which the character uses one of the traits to solve a problem.

absent-minded	enthusiastic	self-reliant
aggressive	happy-go-lucky	sensitive
aloof	hot-headed	serious
bold	humorous	shrewd
bored	idealistic	shy
calm	imaginative	sly
careless	impulsive	realistic
caring	intelligent	resourceful
confident	lazy	rude
conforming	lively	silent
conscientious	loving	stubborn
considerate	mature	talkative
cooperative	passive	tenderhearted
critical	practical	troubled
dull	precise	trusting
easygoing	self-assured	uninhibited

Character Traits

Pick a character from the Single Character Folder. What character traits might this character have that might cause him or her problems? Write a story describing the traits, the problem they caused, and the solution.

absent-minded	enthusiastic	self-reliant
aggressive	happy-go-lucky	sensitive
aloof	hot-headed	serious
bold	humorous	shrewd
bored	idealistic	shy
calm	imaginative	sly
careless	impulsive	realistic
caring	intelligent	resourceful
confident	lazy	rude
conforming	lively	silent
conscientious	loving	stubborn
considerate	mature	talkative
cooperative	passive	tenderhearted
critical	practical	troubled
dull	precise	trusting
easygoing	self-assured	uninhibited

What Can He See?

Choose a picture from the Single Character Folder and examine it closely. What might the character in the picture be able to see that you can't see? Make a list of all the many, unusual things this character might be seeing. Pick one from your list and draw it. Then, write a description of what you have drawn, using as many details as you can.

Into Your World

Choose a picture from the Single Character Folder. What if this character stepped out of the picture and into your life? What might happen? Write a story about it. Make sure your story includes a conflict and a solution.

What Are They Saying?

Look through the pictures in the Multiple Characters Folder. Think about what the people or animals in the picture might be saying. Choose one picture and write a conversation between the people or animals. Make sure to punctuate the conversation correctly and remember to start a new line each time you change speakers. Indent each new line and use quotation marks and commas correctly (e.g., "I love to write," she said.).

Conflicts

Look through the pictures in the Multiple Characters Folder. Pick one. Brainstorm a conflict that two of the characters in the picture might have and write a story about it.

Remember: Every good story has a conflict and a resolution. Be sure you include both of these in your story.

Mix and Match

Look through the pictures in the Settings Folder. Read the story types listed below and choose a story type and match it to a setting. Write a story in the style you have chosen that takes place in the setting you have chosen.

Story type list:

1. an adventure story
2. a holiday story
3. a scary story
4. a Western
5. a science fiction story
6. a ghost story
7. a comedy
8. a fairy tale
9. a tragedy
10. a real-life story

Oh, What a Plot!

Look through the pictures in the setting folder. Read over the possible plots list below and choose a plot and match it to a setting. Write a story that takes place in your chosen setting and follows the plot idea you selected.

Possible plots list:

1. a lost dog
2. a shipwreck
3. a raging blizzard
4. a fire
5. an unexpected visitor
6. a trip back in time
7. a stolen jewel
8. a flat tire
9. a late school bus
10. a contest

Oh No, Not Magic!

Choose a picture from the Setting Folder and examine it closely. Pick one object in the picture. What if this object was magical? And, what if its magic caused a problem? Write a story about the magical object and the problem it caused. Be sure your story includes some kind of resolution to the problem.

Step Into the Setting!

Choose a picture from the Setting Folder and examine it carefully. Then, step into this setting.

- Describe what you see.
- Describe what you smell.
- Describe what you hear.
- Describe what you feel.
- Describe what you taste.

Use your observations about this setting to write a story. Make sure your descriptions paint a picture for the reader.

Fantasy Creatures in Real Places

Many of the characters in a fantasy story are creatures that exist only in the author's imagination. Choose a picture from the setting folder and make up a creature who lives in this place. Describe the creature and tell about its life. Invent a problem or conflict this creature has and how it solves it.

A New Setting

Choose a picture from the Setting Folder and examine it closely. What if your favorite fairy tale took place in this setting? Rewrite the tale and put it in this setting but keep the same characters as they were originally written in the story.

Character/ Setting Inquiry

Pull out a picture from both the Single Character Folder and the Setting Folder. Then, complete these activities, using the pictures as your muse.

1. Put the character in the setting you chose. You will write an adventure, mystery, romance, fairy tale, science fiction, or time travel story about the character in this setting.

2. First, brainstorm a list of words that describe the character. Brainstorm another list that describes the setting.

3. Then, brainstorm a list of reasons why this character might be in this setting.

4. Next, brainstorm a list of problems the character might face while in the setting.

5. Choose one of these problems.

6. Brainstorm a list of solutions. Are there any objects in either picture that might help in the solution? Pick one. Explain how it might help.

7. Now, you are ready to write your story. Refer to your brainstorming lists to guide you as you write.

Where Might You Go?

Choose a picture from the Vehicle Folder and think about where this vehicle might take you. Write a story about an adventure you had on this journey.

Time Travel

Choose a picture from the Vehicle Folder. What if this vehicle was a time machine? Write a story about time travel in this vehicle.

Remember: Every good story has conflict that causes a problem. Be sure that your story has both a problem and a solution.

What's Happening?

A good writer must be a great observer. The writer must notice the things around him or her. Choose a picture from the Event Folder and examine it carefully. Make a list of all of the things that are happening in the picture and write a story about what's happening.

What Might Happen Next?

Choose a picture from the Event Folder. Can you picture what might have happened after the picture was taken? Write a story about it.

What Happened?

Choose a picture from the Event Folder. Think about what might have happened just before the picture was taken and write a story about it.

Student Editing Guide

The essence of writing is the act of rewriting. Even great writers edit and revise their work many times. Good editing requires you to carefully read your work after you have completed it. Follow these steps and learn to be a great editor just like the pros!

Ask These Questions	If "Yes," Follow These Directions . . .
Are there any sentences or paragraphs that are not clear or that do not make sense?	Underline each sentence or paragraph that is unclear.
Are the sentences organized in a logical order in each paragraph?	Place a bracket around the sentences or paragraphs that need to be reorganized.
Does there need to be more description to paint a clearer picture for the reader?	Indicate with a star the sentences or paragraphs that need more description.
Did you use precise words? For example, *gigantic* rather than *big*.	Circle the words that need to be more precise.
Are there any questions you did not answer in the piece? Will your reader want to know more than what you have written?	Make a list of questions that you need to answer to make your piece more complete.

1. If you answered "yes" to any questions, make the necessary changes.
2. Trade papers with a fellow student to check each other's work. Often, it is easier to catch mistakes in others' work than it is in our own!
3. If this paper is to be graded by your teacher, recopy or reprint it after you have made these changes.
4. Remember: All writers need to edit, make changes, and rewrite!

CHAPTER 5

RESEARCH GUIDES AND INDEPENDENT STUDY TASK CARDS

RESEARCH projects can provide an opportunity for all students to learn research skills and grow as independent learners while pursuing a topic of particular interest to them. In addition, bright students who have already mastered a concept and completed unit requirements can be challenged to pursue a topic in depth independently.

Some students are motivated to work on their own and require little direction. These students could develop their own research questions, find necessary resources, and organize their ideas into a well-written product. Most students, however, need more guidance. A structured framework, with questions, activities, and suggested products, is essential for them. It takes time, however, to develop activities like these to guide students in research. The research guide and task cards in this chapter will help you. They were designed to guide students through the research process when working independently. However, even the most self-motivated students will benefit from a teacher-directed overview of the procedures and meetings with teachers to plan and discuss their research. Teachers should set up time to meet at intervals with students, either in small groups or individually, to discuss the progress of their research. The beauty of differentiated learning, especially independent projects, is that it allows for such teacher flexibility.

The Research Folder Strategy student guide (see p. 113) was designed to help students organize their facts and ideas. It also was designed to help students develop note-taking skills and to use their notes to write reports in their own words, not copy word for word from an encyclopedia or directly off of the Internet.

To make research folders, glue six envelopes to the inside of a manila folder and attach a paper clip to each envelope. Hand out the student guide and the research folder. The guide directs students to write a question on a note card and attach that card to an envelope with the paper clip. They are then directed to identify five more pertinent questions, writing each one on a card and attaching it to the other envelopes. Each envelope contains a question.

Students will research each question and write the answers on note cards, filing each card in the envelope behind the appropriate question. When they have answered all of the questions, the information they have gathered on their note cards will guide their writing of a great report.

However, research need not culminate in a conventional written report. The Task Cards for Independent Research (see pp. 116–124) offer students generic topics for independent research, as well as ideas for various kinds of student products to present their findings. There are three sets of cards, each with a different focus for research: inventions, people, and events. The included handouts contain sample topics within each of three categories. These topics can and should be expanded upon by both teacher and students, but are good ideas to get started.

To make the task cards, you will need three large envelopes. Label them: *Inventions, People,* and *Events.* Copy the cards and laminate them or put them in plastic sandwich bags. Place the task cards in the appropriate envelope and use these task cards whenever your students are working on independent projects.

The Research Folder Strategy: Ten Steps to a Great Research Project: A Student Guide

Follow these steps to write a detailed, interesting research paper.

1. Choose a topic to research.

2. Write everything you already know about this topic on index cards or a sheet of notebook paper. Then, write down all of the things you think you know about this topic, but are not certain are correct.

3. Make a list of questions you have about your research topic. Try to think of questions that are *open-ended*, questions that cannot be answered with just one or two words. For example, this is an open-ended question on the topic of the Wright brothers: *What were the Wright brothers like when they were boys?* This question begs for details. This is a *one-word answer* question: *Where were the Wright brothers born?* Few, if any, details are required to answer this.

4. Choose three good open-ended questions and write them on note cards. Clip the cards to the envelopes in the folder—one question per card and one card per envelope.

5. Research the questions. Use a variety of resources to help you find the answers to the questions. As you read, jot down facts on index cards— one fact per card—that give details regarding the questions. You do not have to write complete sentences on the cards. You may write down only one word, or a phrase. For example: *How did they get interested in flight? (Card #1: Worked on bikes in bike shop; Card #2: Fascinated with flight of birds).* Put all of these cards inside the envelope for this question. Then, turn your attention to the question on the next envelope and repeat the directions in Step 5.

6. Organize your research into a logical order. Focus on the question on the first envelope. Pull out all of the cards from that envelope and lay them down on your desk. Read the facts on each card. Think about how the facts fit together and put all related facts into a stack. You need to consider *sequence* (order) and *general-to-specific* facts when ordering the cards. After you arranged all of the note cards from Envelope 1, put

them in a stack and clip them together. Then, arrange the next group of facts in the next envelope.

7. After you have arranged all of the facts in each stack, it is time to arrange all of your stacks into a logical order for your written report. How can you arrange the questions you have answered into an order that makes sense? Is it better to organize your questions chronologically (ordered in time)? Does it make more sense to give the most interesting information first? Your teacher can help you in making this decision.

8. Write the report.
   - First, write an introduction. This will be your first paragraph. It should be a short paragraph that tells readers what they will learn about as they read your report. It typically is a general statement about your topic. The introduction can begin with a fact, a question, or a quote. For example: *The Wright brothers played an important role in the history of aviation.*
   - Next, focus on the question you have chosen to begin with. Using the facts you gathered about it, write a topic sentence to introduce the paragraph. This sentence summarizes all of the facts pertaining to the question. For example, if your first paragraph was about the Wright brothers' childhood, a topic sentence could be: *Orville and Wilbur Wright were curious about everything when they were young.*
   - Next, turn the facts you jotted down on each card into sentences. After you have finished sentences for your first question, focus on the second question. Keep going until you have answered all of the questions on your envelopes. Remember to begin a new paragraph with each one.

9. Write the *conclusion*. Now you are ready to write the last paragraph. It summarizes in two or three sentences the main idea or point of your report. For example: *The Wright brothers made one of the most important contributions in the field of transportation. Their influence on our world is still felt today more than 100 years after their first flight in Kitty Hawk.*

10. Edit and revise. Reread your report. Make certain that you thoroughly answered all of the questions. Also, edit for grammatical errors. Trade papers with a classmate and edit each other's paper. Revise your report and write the final draft.

Topics for Independent Research—Inventions

Choose One of These Inventions to Study	
Bicycles	Microscopes
Cars	X-ray
Trains	MRI
Airplanes	Vaccines
Sea-going ships	Iron lung for polio victims
Submarines	Eyeglasses
Rockets into space	False teeth
Radio	Board games
Television	Video games
Cameras	Toys
Telephones	Toy trains
Computers	Football
CDs	Tennis racket
Or, choose any other invention or scientific discovery that interests you. Then, complete one or more of the task cards regarding this invention.	

How Has This Invention Changed Over Time?

1. Find out how this invention has changed over time.
2. Predict how it might continue to change or develop over the next 100 years. Examine the patterns in its development in the past as clues to future developments.

Now, show the changes in A and B in one of the following:

- Timeline
- Comic book
- Mock interview with the inventor
- Autobiography of the invention (written from its point of view)

What Else Was Going On?

Find out what was going on in the world at the time this was invented.
For example:

- Who was President of the United States?
- What important world events were happening?
- What was the lifestyle of the average American citizen like at that time?
- Who were the famous people of the day? Why were they famous?
- What were other important inventions or discoveries made within 5 years of that time?

Share your findings in one of the following ways:

- Timeline
- Mobile
- Newspaper

What Makes It Tick?

How does this invention work? What are its important parts?

Show your findings in one of the following:

- Diagram or series of diagrams
- Model
- Entry in an encyclopedia

What Made Them Do It?

- Make a list of people who played an important role in the development of this invention. Include the earliest inventors and those people who made significant changes to it.
- Read biographies and newspaper, magazine, and Internet articles about some of these people.
- In addition to the usual biographical information, try to uncover why they were interested in this invention and what obstacles they might have faced when working on the invention.

Show your findings in one of the following:

- Autobiography (written as if you were one of the inventors)
- A series of letters written by one or more of these inventors
- Box museum about the inventors

Who Benefited From This Invention?

- Who was most likely to benefit from this invention? Explain.
- Who might not care about or even like this invention? Explain.
- Who would have profited from this invention? List all those who profited from it and explain how and why they profited.

Demonstrate your ideas in one of the following:

- Comic book (about one who profited or one who disliked the invention)
- Letter to the editor of a newspaper (written by one of those who either profited or disliked the invention)
- Magazine advertisement

Topics for Independent Research—People

Choose One of These People to Research	
Elvis Presley	A president
Princess Diana	A dictator
Stephen King	A famous athlete
R. L. Stine	An Olympic gold medalist
Madeleine L'Engle	A TV star
Vincent van Gogh	A famous explorer
Mozart	A famous astronaut
John F. Kennedy	A famous inventor
Martin Luther King, Jr.	A famous artist or composer
King Arthur	A famous writer
Mother Teresa	Any other person who interests you
Complete one or more of the task cards regarding this person.	

What Would You Like to Ask?

1. After reading a bit about the person you have chosen to research, brainstorm a list of questions you would like to ask him or her. Make certain that you have questions regarding all of the major areas of a person's life (including childhood, work, family, and interests).

2. Research to find the answers to your questions. If there are any you cannot find answers to, choose another question to research.

3. Show your findings in one of the following products:
   - Timeline
   - Autobiography (written as if you were the person you are researching)
   - Scrapbook of a person's life (replicas of important documents, birth certificates, diplomas, pictures, letters, and so on).

Who Else Was Famous?

1. Make a list of other people who were famous in the world at the same time the person you're researching was famous.

2. Star those people who might have influenced your person. Now, make a list of people who were not necessarily famous but who influenced the person you're researching.

3. Choose one other person from either list and explain their influence on the person.

Show your findings in one of the following products:
   - A written conversation between the two people
   - Two letters written from one to the other
   - Comic strip about these two people with dialogue between them

What Was Going On in the World?

1. Make a list of important events that were occurring in the world at the time the person you're researching was famous.

2. Put a star by those events that were significant to the person you're researching.

3. Choose one event that you starred and explain why it was significant and how it affected the person you're researching.

Show your findings in one of the following products:

- Diary entry or entries about the event written by the person you're researching
- Drawing illustrating the person's reaction to the event
- Diorama illustrating the event

Task Cards for Independent Research—Events

Choose One of These Events to Research	
The Boston Tea Party	The Great Depression
California gold rush	The orphan trains
Lewis and Clark expedition	Dolly, the cloned sheep
The Trail of Tears	Invasion of Normandy in WWII
The sinking of the Titanic	The birth of Hollywood
Mapping the human genome	The space race
The Mexican Revolution	The Korean War
The first personal computer	Polio epidemic in 1950s
1929 stock market crash	The race riots of the 1960s

Or, choose any other event that interests you. Then, complete one or more of the task cards regarding this event.

Why Did This Event Make History?

1. Read about the event, using a variety of resources and list the reasons this event made history.

2. Then, take notes of things that led up to this event or why this event happened.

3. Next, make a list of people who were affected by the event. Explain how they were affected and why.

Demonstrate your findings in one of these products:

- A monument honoring those who were affected by this event
- A timeline illustrating this event
- Lyrics to a song or a poem about this event.

What Else Was Going On in the World?

1. Make a list of other important events that were occurring in the world at the time this event was happening.

2. Choose one of these events and find out why it was so important.

3. Did this event influence the event you're researching? If so, how and why?

Make a Venn diagram of this event and the one you're researching to explore their similarities and differences.

What Happened as a Result of This Event?

1. Research the effects of this event on history.
2. Make a list of other events that happened because of the one you're researching.
3. Rank order these other events. Put #1 by the event that was most important, #2 by the second most important, and so on.
4. Now, think "What If?" What if the event you're researching had never happened? How might things be different in our world today? Make a list of your ideas.

Illustrate your ideas in one of these products:
- A series of newspaper headlines
- A story about this different world
- A Venn diagram comparing and contrasting this different world and the world as it is now

Consider the Event From Different Points of View

1. Read to find out who was in favor of the event and who was opposed.
2. Make a table with two columns. List people in favor of the event in the first column and list those who were opposed in the second. For example, the British King, the East India Company, and the Mohawk Indians would have opposed the Boston Tea Party. On the other hand, the Patriot colonists were in favor of it.

Choose one person or group from both columns. List the reasons they were either for or against the event. Demonstrate your findings in one of these products:
- A cartoon illustrating a debate between the two groups
- A series of letters written from one person in favor to his cousin who was against the event
- An argument for or against honoring this event on the anniversary of its occurrence every year

CHAPTER 6
PRODUCT LISTS AND RUBRICS

PRODUCTS, the result of those projects you assign at the end of units or chapters, provide an excellent vehicle for differentiation. You can differentiate products in several ways: you might vary the complexity of the task required, vary the type of product, or allow students to choose their products.

When you want to differentiate, choose products from the product list (see Table 6). It is divided into four categories: products students write, draw/design, construct, or present. It is important for students to produce products from each category throughout the school year. In that way, they will learn to communicate their ideas in a variety of ways.

Students come to you with different talents and learning styles. As a result, they might be excited more by one product type than another. For example, students with kinesthetic aptitudes typically prefer products requiring construction and will be attracted to this type of product. If given a choice, they might always choose a product they can construct. For this reason, you may want to allow student choice only occasionally. When you do allow it, pick two or three products from which they can choose.

When determining the product types to assign, consider the following questions:

- What is the content of the unit or chapter? The main concept? The key ideas?
- What product types would best enable students to demonstrate what they know about this content?
- What production talents and abilities do my students already exhibit?
- What production skills and abilities do my students need to develop?

Table 6
Product Lists

Write	Draw/Design	Construct	Present
20-card fact file	Album cover	Aquarium	Composition
Advertisement	Banner	Artifact box	Dance
Autobiography	Billboard	Board game	Display
Book report	Blueprint	Card game	Mime
Chart	Book jacket	Costume	Play a musical instrument
Diary	Booklet	Diorama	Rap
Editorial	Brochure	Experiment	Role-play
Essay	Bulletin board	Habitat	Skit
Fable	Cartoon	Invention	Song
Journal	Chart	Jigsaw puzzle	Speech
Limerick	Collage	Machine	Story-telling
Logic puzzle	Crossword puzzle	Mobile	Videotape
Myth	Diagram	Model	
News article	Display	Monument	
Outline	Flow chart	Musical instrument	
Play	Flipbook	Origami	
Poem	Graph	Relief map	
Puppet show	Greeting card		
Questionnaire	Illustration		
Quiz	Magazine ad		
Recipe book	Map		
Script	Museum collection		
Scroll	Newspaper		
Skit	Pamphlet		
Song lyric	Patent		
Story	Postage stamp		
Survey	Poster		
TV script	Scrapbook		
Worksheet	Stand-up cutouts		
	Travel log		
	Timeline		
	Weather map		
	Web		
	Word search		

Authentic assessment is a critical component of product evaluation. Four generic rubrics are provided on pages 128–131. These are tools for this type of assessment that will enable you to be more objective when evaluating a product that is typically measured subjectively.

Students produce a better product if they know beforehand the criteria that will be used in its evaluation. When you give an assignment to your students, hand out a copy of the rubric you will use. Discuss the criteria, clarifying any questions students might have. In doing this, students must assume responsibility for their work and their grade. "Why did you give me this grade?" becomes a question they can no longer ask. They know what is expected before they take even the first step to create their product.

There are four types of rubrics in this chapter, one for each product category. Each rubric contains generic criteria appropriate for the different categories and can be used in assessing all of the products listed on the product lists. On page 132 you will find an explanation of the criteria levels for the rubrics, as well as words to describe these qualitative levels. The conversion table that follows will help you convert the total scores to percentiles.

Date: _____

Rubric: Written Product

Areas to Be Scored	Criteria for Each Area	Scoring Key 4 = Excellent 3 = Above Average 2 = Average 1 = Below Average 0 = Incomplete
Content	**Written text (report, story, etc.)**	**Score**
	Introduction defines the subject, purpose, and/or problem.	
	Text includes details to explain, describe, or illustrate key ideas, issues, and facts.	
	Closing presents problem solution, draws conclusions, and/or summarizes ideas.	
	Text includes evidence to explain solutions and support conclusions.	
	Text is appropriate for intended audience.	
	Total Score	
Composition	**How the text is written (mechanics)**	**Score**
	Key ideas, issues, and facts are well organized (introduction, body, closing).	
	Varied sentence structure adds interest to text.	
	Advanced vocabulary is used in text.	
	Punctuation, grammar, and spelling rules are followed in text.	
	Style is consistent throughout piece.	
	Total Score	
Creativity	**Thinking out of the box**	**Score**
	Topic is presented from an unusual/unique point of view (perspective).	
	Descriptive language is used in text (e.g., vivid nouns, adjectives).	
	Elaboration is used in text and/or illustrations.	
	Metaphors are used to define, describe, and illustrate key ideas, issues, and facts.	
	Text and graphics are presented in dramatic way (use of 3-D, borders, etc.).	
	Total Score	
Graphics (If Used)	**Illustrations, diagrams, graphs, photographs**	**Score**
	Graphics illustrate or symbolize key ideas, facts, or issues.	
	Graphics are located in logical place within the text.	
	Graphics are large enough to see.	
	Graphics are arranged in attractive manner (negative space surrounds text, pictures).	
	Graphics are neat (cut out, glued, colored, painted, etc.).	
	Total Score	
Total	**Highest Possible Score: 80 (With Graphics) 60 (Without Graphics)**	
	Total Score in All Areas	

See Conversion Table to convert score from Total Score to percentage and letter grade.	**% Score**	
	Letter Grade	

Rubric: Drawn or Designed Product

Areas to Be Scored	Criteria for Each Area	Scoring Key 4 = Excellent 3 = Above Average 2 = Average 1 = Below Average 0 = Incomplete

Content	Written text (report, story, etc.)	Score
	Text includes relevant facts, ideas, and issues about topic.	
	Text includes details to explain, describe, or illustrate key ideas, issues, and facts.	
	Key ideas, issues, and facts are well organized.	
	Punctuation, grammar, and spelling rules are used in text.	
	Text is appropriate for intended audience.	
	Total Score	

Visuals	Graphics (pictures, drawings, photographs, etc.) or objects	Score
	Collectively, visuals convey main point or idea of project.	
	Each visual illustrates or symbolizes a relevant idea, fact, or issue.	
	Visuals are arranged in attractive manner (negative space surrounds text, pictures).	
	Visuals are cut out and glued into place neatly.	
	Visuals are large enough to see.	
	Total Score	

Creativity	Thinking out of the box	Score
	Topic is presented from an unusual or unique point of view (perspective).	
	Descriptive language is used in text (e.g., vivid nouns, adjectives).	
	Elaboration is used in text and/or illustrations (many details).	
	Text is presented in dramatic way (unusual fonts, use of glitter, borders, etc.)	
	Graphics are presented in dramatic way (use of 3-D, borders, etc.)	
	Total Score	

Total	Highest Possible Score: 60	
	Total Score in All Areas	

See Conversion Table to convert score from Total Score to percentage and letter grade.	% Score	
	Letter Grade	

Name: _____ **Date:** _____

Rubric: Constructed Product

Areas to Be Scored	Criteria for Each Area	Scoring Key
		4 = Excellent 3 = Above Average 2 = Average 1 = Below Average 0 = Incomplete

Model	Model or object produced	Score
	Purpose of model is clear.	
	Model demonstrates knowledge of subject being studied.	
	Model is realistic.	
	Model is within teacher guidelines for project.	
	Total Score	

Construction	How model is made	Score
	Model is well put together (does not easily fall apart).	
	Size of model is appropriate.	
	Parts of model are proportionate in size to other parts.	
	Model is attractive, neat.	
	Total Score	

Creativity	Thinking out of the box	Score
	Materials used to make model are clever or unique.	
	Model is unusual, eye-catching.	
	Elaboration is used in model (details are added that are not required).	
	Model is presented from an unusual or unique point of view (perspective).	
	Total Score	

Total	Highest Possible Score: 48	
	Total Score in All Areas	

See Conversion Table to convert score from Total Score to percentage and letter grade.	% Score	
	Letter Grade	

Rubric: Presented Product

Areas to Be Scored	Criteria for Each Area	Scoring Key 4 = Excellent 3 = Above Average 2 = Average 1 = Below Average 0 = Incomplete

Content	Topic	Score
	Key facts, ideas, and issues of topic are introduced and/or problem is stated.	
	Key facts, ideas, and issues are explained, described, and/or summarized.	
	Conclusions are drawn about topic and/or problem solution is presented.	
	Evidence to support conclusion or solution is presented.	
	Organization of content is logical.	
	Total Score	

Body Language	Performance	Score
	Student looks at audience during presentation.	
	Student stands straight and is still.	
	Student speaks without stumbling or pausing.	
	Student speaks loudly.	
	Student speaks slowly, distinctly.	
	Total Score	

Creativity	Thinking out of the box	Score
	Topic is presented from an unusual/unique point of view (perspective).	
	Eye-catching visuals illustrate and/or support key ideas, facts, and issues.	
	Effects not required added to presentation (costumes, props, sound effects, etc.).	
	Student speaks with expression, sense of drama.	
	Student uses humor in presentation.	
	Total Score	

Total	Highest Possible Score: 60	
	Total Score in All Areas	

See Conversion Table to convert score from Total Score to percentage and letter grade.	% Score	
	Letter Grade	

Words to Describe Qualitative Levels for Each Criteria Item

Excellent
4 Points

All
Criteria completely met.
Product is completely thorough.
All items are complete.
Demonstrates criteria 3 or more times (when criteria can be measured quantitatively).

Above Average
3 Points

Most
Criteria almost completely met.
Most items are complete (e.g., all except 1 or 2).
Demonstrates criteria 3 times (when criteria can be measured quantitatively).

Average
2 Points

Some
Criteria somewhat met.
Some items are complete (e.g., all except 3–5).
Demonstrates criteria twice (when criteria can be measured quantitatively).

Below Average
1 Point

Few
Criteria barely met.
Product is not thorough.
Most items are incomplete.
Demonstrates criteria once (when criteria can be measured quantitatively).

Incomplete
0 Points

None
All items are incomplete.
Product does not meet criteria.

One Possible Conversion
From
% Score
to
Letter Grade

A++ = 100
A+ = 98
A = 95
A- = 92
B+ = 88
B = 85
B- = 82
C+ = 78
C = 75
C- = 72
D+ = 68
D = 65
D- = 62
F = 55

To figure percentage, divide total number of points earned by total number of points possible.

Multiply by 100 to get percentage.

Conversion Table
(From Total Score to Percentiles)

Total Score	%	Total Score	%	Total Score	%	Total Score	%	Total Score	%
80 Highest	100	21	26	60 Highest	100	48 Highest	100	40 High	100
79	99	20	25	59	98	47	98	39	98
78	98	19	23	58	97	46	96	38	95
77	96	18	22	57	95	45	94	37	93
76	95	17	21	56	93	44	92	36	90
75	94	16	20	54	90	43	90	35	88
74	93	15	18	53	88	42	88	34	85
73	91	14	17	52	87	41	86	33	83
72	90	13	16	51	85	40	84	32	80
71	89	12	15	50	83	39	82	31	78
70	88	11	12	49	82	38	80	30	75
69	86	10	12	48	80	37	78	29	73
68	85	9	10	47	78	36	76	28	70
67	83	8	9	46	77	35	73	27	68
66	82	7	8	45	75	34	71	26	65
65	81	6	6	44	73	33	69	25	63
64	80	5	5	43	72	32	67	24	60
63	79	4	4	42	70	31	65	23	58
62	78	3	2	41	68	30	63	23	55
61	76	2	1	40	67	29	60	21	53
60	75	1	1	39	65	28	58	20	50
59	74	0	0	38	63	27	56	19	48
58	73			37	62	26	54	18	45
57	71			36	60	25	52	17	43
56	70			35	58	24	50	16	40
55	69			34	57	23	48	15	38
54	68			33	55	22	46	14	35
53	66			32	53	21	44	13	33
52	65			31	52	20	42	12	30
51	64			30	50	19	40	11	28
50	63			29	48	18	38	10	25
49	61			28	47	17	36	9	23
48	60			27	45	16	34	8	20
47	59			26	43	15	32	7	18
46	58			25	42	14	30	6	15
45	56			24	40	13	27	5	13
44	55			23	38	12	25	4	10
43	54			22	37	11	23	3	8
42	53			21	35	10	21	2	5
41	51			20	33	9	19	1	3
40	50			19	32	8	17		
39	49			18	30	7	15		
38	48			17	28	6	13		
37	46			16	27	5	10		
36	45			15	25	4	8		
35	43			14	23	3	6		
34	42			13	22	2	4		
33	41			12	20	1	2		
32	40			11	18				
31	38			10	16				
30	37			9	15				
29	36			8	13				
28	35			7	12				
27	33			6	10				
26	32			5	8				
25	31			4	7				
24	30			3	5				
23	28			2	3				
22	28			1	2				

REFERENCES

Eeds, M., & Wells, D. (1989). Grand conversations: An exploration of meaning construction in literature study groups. *Research in the Teaching of English, 23,* 4-29.

Peterson, R., & Eeds, M. (1990). *Grand conversations: Literature groups in action.* New York: Scholastic.

Thompkins, G. (1997). *Literacy for the 21st century.* Upper Saddle River, NJ: Prentice Hall.

RESOURCES FOR SUGGESTED READING

Armstrong, T. (2002). *You're smarter than you think! A kid's guide to multiple intelligences.* Minneapolis, MN: Free Spirit.

Coil, C. (2004). *Standards-based activities and assessments for the differentiated classroom.* Marion, OH: Pieces of Learning.

Diller, D. (2005). *Practice with purpose: Literacy work stations for grades 3–6.* Markham, Ontario: Stenhouse.

Dodge, J. (2005). *Differentiation in action: A complete resource with research-supported strategies to help you plan and organize differentiated instruction—and achieve success with all learners.* New York: Scholastic.

Dunn, R., & Dunn, K. (1992). *Teaching elementary students through their individual learning styles: Practical approaches for grades 3–6.* Needham Heights, MA: Allyn & Bacon.

Heacox, D. (2002). *Differentiating instruction in the regular classroom: How to reach and teach all learners, grades 3–12.* Minneapolis, MN: Free Spirit.

Jenson, E. (1998) *Teaching with the brain in mind.* Alexandria, VA: Association for Supervision and Curriculum Development.

Kingore, B. (2004). *Differentiation: Simplified, realistic, and effective.* Austin, TX: Professional Associates Publishing.

Roberts, J. L., & Inman, T. F. (2009). *Strategies for differentiating instruction: Best practices for the classroom* (2nd ed.). Waco, TX: Prufrock Press.

Tomlinson, C. A. (1999). *The differentiated classroom: Responding to the needs of all learners.* Alexandria, VA: Association for Supervision and Curriculum Development.

Tomlinson, C. A. (2001). *How to differentiate instruction in mixed-ability classrooms* (2nd ed.). Alexandria, VA: Association for Supervision and Curriculum Development.

Tomlinson, C. A. (2003). *Differentiation in practice: A resource guide for differentiating curriculum, grades 5–9.* Alexandria, VA: Association for Supervision and Curriculum Development.

Tomlinson, C. A. (2003). *Fulfilling the promise of the differentiated classroom: Strategies and tools for responsive teaching.* Alexandria, VA: Association for Supervision and Curriculum Development.

Tomlinson, C. A., Brimijoin, K., & Narvaez, L. (2008). *The differentiated school: Making revolutionary changes in teaching and learning.* Alexandria, VA: Association for Supervision and Curriculum Development.

Tomlinson, C., & McTighe, J. (2006). *Integrating differentiated instruction & understanding by design: Connecting content and kids.* Alexandria, VA: Association for Supervision and Curriculum Development.

Wiggins, G., & McTighe, J. (1998). *Understanding by design.* Alexandria, VA: Association for Supervision and Curriculum Development.

Winebrenner, S. (2001). *Teaching gifted kids in the regular classroom: Strategies and techniques every teacher can use to meet the academic needs of the gifted and talented.* Minneapolis, MN: Free Spirit.

ABOUT THE AUTHOR

AN educator for 27 years, Mary Ann Carr has taught grades K–7. In addition to working in the classroom, she was a resource teacher for a Chapter 1 program in an inner-city school and a gifted specialist in a large suburban school system. This wide range of experience provided the seed for her passion for differentiation and her understanding of issues facing teachers out in the trenches.

Carr found that teachers generally lack two things—time and materials. Taking into account these and other concerns voiced by teachers, Carr began developing instructional materials to make their jobs easier. Frequently asked to present in workshops and at state conferences, she promotes differentiation through humorous and motivational presentations that provide practical tools teachers can use to meet the diverse needs of their students.

Carr is the author of *One-Hour Mysteries*, *More One-Hour Mysteries*, *The Private Eye School*, and *The Great Chocolate Caper*, all published by Prufrock Press. These CSI-like mysteries require students to engage in critical thinking while having fun solving crimes in the classroom.